Before I Start

It is said that each of us has at least one book in them. This is mine.

As I have grown older I have realised that even though we live in a celebrity driven world, a world that is often shallow and driven by greed and selfishness, one thing remains as true today as it always has, basically, people are interested in people. Sometimes we just wish to escape into someone elses life for a minute. Perhaps they are wealthy or beautiful, live in an exotic place or lead a life that is beyond our wildest dream. Othertimes, we are just curious or even plain nosy. No matter how close to someone, we only know what we see or "experience" of them. So much of them is tucked away in their head.

We all live in a highly developed world and are overloaded by internet information on every conceivable subject. Yet, in this information superhighway there is still room for a book – a good novel, a travel story, whatever. My passion is reading about people's lives. Some of my greatest reads have not been written about superstars but about or by ordinary people about their ordinary lives.

Todays world is one of eMails, text messages and digital photographs, gone are the

Before I Start

records created by letter writing, diaries and photograph albums. Communication is oft of temporary record and technology makes electronic information obsolete at an alarming speed.

As I have gotten older I have realised how the memories of everyday folk matter to the next generation. If ordinary people do not document their ordinary lives much will be lost of our times. It is my hope that long after I have gone, my future descendants will have an insight into my life way beyond that I ever had into my own fathers.

My book is about my life. Like most human beings, my ordinary life has been populated by some extraordinary people. That doesn't mean they were famous, just that in the context of my life, "extraordinary". It is also about my experiences, extraordinary only because they are diffferent to yours, the reader. My choice of words is deliberate. If something is not ordinary, then by my definition it is extra ordinary. My friends and family think that being a One Man Band is not ordinary, driving donkeys is not ordinary, working in a laundry is not ordinary.

It is these "not ordinary" things I have written about.

Before I Start

To put this record of my life into a context I have to dedicate it to those people who have been fundamental to the course it took.

My parents, Albert and Marjorie Ellen, came from diferent parts of England. My dad, a Mancunian, came from Eccles, Manchester. He first worked at Irlam Steel Works during which time he went to night school to study City and Guilds in industrial design. The Woodhead family was large. Dad had a twin brother Fred (who drowned in a canal) and several other brothers and sisters. I remember my Aunt & Uncle having a fish and chip shop on Regent Street, Eccles. I remember occasional family visits to Eccles and marvelling at the big ships that still worked the canal.

My Mom, born a Broadhead, longed to marry a Smith or a Jones. She never planned to marry anyone with a strange name and Woodhead is uncannily similar to Broadhead. When she met Albert, my dad, they were

Before I Start

both in Blackpool on holiday. Blackpool in the war years was THE resort of the north and Midlands probably because it was easy to access via an excellent rail infrastucture. My dad would have travelled from Manchester whilst my mom probably went directly from Bilston station. Dad was on leave from the RAF and would have been resplendent in RAF blue. Early photographs shows the RAF wings on his collar but he left the RAF due to a hearing impairment.

He eventually spent the war years in a reserved occupation (manufacturing for the war effort) and like many served in "Dads Army" the Home Guard. His only firearm was a wooden rifle and with that he spent his nights guarding Ringway Airfield, now Manchester Airport, from Nazi paratroop attack. My dad was an intelligent man, quietly spoken with delicate hands and fingers. He played the harmonica, comb and paper and spoons. He spent his life in the roll turning industry (where red hot steel ingots are "turned" into semi or finished product). Dad had been a boxer during his National Service and could be handy if

Before I Start

needed. Mom would tell a story about him giving his boss a good hiding then throwing into the canal that runs alongside Cable Street, Wolverhampton. I only ever remember him losing his temper twice. On the first occasion he blockaded himself in the front room and chopped the furniture up (perhaps it was a choice between the furniture or my mother, who knows). On the second occasion, he threw my cousins from Manchester out of our house in Bilston. They had been researching the Woodhead family tree. My dad remembered his father, my Grandad Woodhead as a sole parent who singlehandedly provided for and brought up the large family. He was a bible reading man. My cousins were to advise my dad that his father was a womaniser and drinker. He would have none of it. They were quickly despatched back to Manchester. I have no idea what relatives I have in Manchester. I always believe that my mother chose to distance herself and my dad from them. I may be wrong in that but certainly my legacy is that I have no idea who is alive and little idea of whoever lived bearing the name Woodhead.

My dad was an example to his children. He didn't go to the pub. In fact he rarely drank, didn't much like the taste (I take after him in this respect). He was very practical and

Before I Start

could turn his hand to anything – household maintenance, gardening, building, cobbling and toy making to name but few (I take after him in that too). He was hard working, honest and clean living. He liked a smoke but then his generation was brought up on cheap or even free tobacco as part of their military remuneration. As a young boy, he was my hero in very simple ways. He could bite into an ice cream wafer with his teeth and I couldn't! I didn't know then that his teeth were false as he had them all taken out aged 21 because he suffered a gum disorder called piorhea.

My mom, Ellen Marjorie , was born in Bilston and as a child lived in Windsor St, next to the cemetery. She went to Ettingshall (Tin) School and later worked at Edges Shoe factory on Wellington Road, Bilston. She was told that her father had been killed in the first World War. That was not the case. He appears to have run off with another woman. Mom was a stunning blonde in her wedding photographs. She

Before I Start

had slightly protruding teeth (she was always fearful that her children would have them too but none of us did), but that never averted ones gaze from her beauty. She was always beautifiul even later in life with age. She was passionate about her hair and spent hours putting it into place. She was a strong willed and very single minded woman with astounding foresight. She liked or disliked a person in seconds and was, to my knowledge, never wrong. Mom was the driver of the family fortune. It was she who wanted. As a child we moved house four times, each time to improve the family fortune. It was she who decided the car should be sold & replaced. Her relationship with my dad worked very well because he would do anything for an easy life. He suffered his first heart trouble early in life and perhaps that was why he never sought to find conflict in his middle to late life. My mom never stopped working. She held down various jobs throughout her life and always worked - shoe maker, cleaner, telephonist, shop assistant, post office clerk, post office manager. She brought up three sons of which I am the middle one. She had a terrific work ethic and never shirked or took short cuts. She was as dependable an employee as anyone could have. I never remember her being too ill to work and early in my life, dad would come in from work at

Before I Start

the factory and mom would go out to work evenings at the telephone exchange. My mum wasn't much of a cook. My love of thin runny gravy results from her failure to ever manage the skill of gravy making. I have few memories of family meals and except for Sundays don't recall sit down meals (except at my nans). A piece (sandwich) on the pavement or a slice of "dipbread" (bread dipped in lard or fat) is my most vivid culinary memory. She might not have been a good cook but my, was she a dancer. She would wear my dad out at his annual Christmas dinner from his employer , George Gadds of Tipton. It was usually held at The Stewponey in Stourbridge and was obviously a family affair as I remember going there.

I never knew my Grandad Charles Woodhead, but my mom was daughter to Elizabeth Broadhead. Elizabeth, or Nellie as she was known became housekeeper to Charles Turner who owned a spring works in Wolverhampton (J H Turner & Son Ltd). My nan "lived in" to look after him and my mom was brought up regarding Charlie as her surrogate father. We all called him Uncle Charlie, oddly, so did she. As a child I remember him owning a big black Wolseley car complete with running board. After that it was a Rover 95. He would take me to his

Before I Start

spring works in Horseley Fields, Wolverhampton on a Saturday morning and weigh me on the industrial scales. I never knew him to drive in excess of 20mph, usually with two wheels either side of the white line (there was little traffic then). I also remember him taking me to Pattingham to view a pig! His hands were twisted with arthritis and he wore special boots because his toes were also mishapen by the illness. He always wore a suit with waistcoat and watch fob and a trilby hat. I never recall seeing him casually dressed. Earlier in his life, his passion had been crown green bowling and I recall playing with his bowls as a child. JH Turner Ltd manufactured springs and during the war had been part of the war effort manufacuring for grenades, rifles and other armamants. With lack of petrol for civilian purposes, it was said that Uncle Charlie would wheelbarrow springs from Horseley Fields, Wolverhampton, to Willenhall (6 or 7 miles each way).

My nan and her home on Wellington Road, Bilston, played a big part in my life as a child. The house was in what was once the "elegant" part of Bilston. It was big with a cavernous hallway and a sweeping staircase. The back garden must have approached an acre and my nan tended it singlehandedly growing all variety of vegetables and fruit.

Before I Start

Rhubarb was her speciality and I remember their thick red stalks and large dark green leaves with absolute clarity. I have always remembered lying in my pram, in Nans back garden. I would of course be a baby so it is possible that I imagined it. Nonetheless it is an image I have been able to visualise all my life. At the end of the garden were large double gates, probably 15ft high and probably at least as wide. Also at the end of the garden was Uncle Charlies concrete air raid shelter once crammed with army surplus – tin hats, grenade casings and other things that I did not recognize. Nan & Uncle Charlies house was en route from my home on Millfields Road (opposite Stewart and Lloyds) to Ettingshall Primary School in Hall Park Street. From home, my elder brother Keith would cycle and I would scoot (on my scooter), down Chem Road, across the railway, past the shop and the gas lamp and down the alley. We would then be opposite Hickman Park. Turning left we would then go across the railway again with a final descent to 194, Wellington Road; downhill all the way. We would then deposit our transport in my nans garage and walk on to school.

At lunchtime (dinner we called it, probably because it was called dinnertime at school), we would walk back to nans for my dinner.

Before I Start

Always hot, it would have been the purpose of her morning and was always designed to fill. Whatever it was, would have been created in a huge black open fire and cooking range which took up half of one wall in the kitchen. She would get it going each morning with wood and coal and "draw" it with a newspaper stretched across the open fire front. Occasionally this would catch fire, but not often. There were always lots of vegetables especially potatoes. There was always a pudding – rice pudding (with jam), jam roly poly or other home made pastry based creations. Dinner was always at table and the table always had a white cotton tablecloth over a maroon, brown or green underlay. Uncle Charlie would sometimes return home for lunch and always had his own chair in the kitchen which no one else sat on. The kitchen was big enough to house a three piece suite and anyone else had to sit on the settee or in my case, on his knee. After lunch, we would all chat or perhaps listen to the BBC Light Programme which would have been broadcasting Workers Playtime. If my Uncle Charlie was home from the factory, he would always have his own meal usually of traditional foods that seemed old fashioned to me – cows heel, pigs trotters, heart, eel. In fact much of his diet would today be described as offal. I didn't know it but

Before I Start

already the culinary tastes of the generations had changed and would continue to do so throughout my lifetime.

I remember my Uncle Charlie dying. I loved him dearly as any child should love their "grandad". His death had a profound effect on me. My nan lived on into old age and eventually lived with my Aunt and Uncle. She was a sprightly old stick but eventually succumbed to smoking too many Woodbines plus of course the passage of time.

At least once a week my Aunty Edith would come for dinner at nans. She worked as a book keeper at a glass factory in Wolverhampton on the main road to Bilston (one bus journey). Aunty Edith was mother to my cousin Roy. They lived in Fallings Park, Wolverhampton. Aunty Edith was married to Uncle Ken. He came from Sheffield, the home of stainless steel, and like my own father worked in the steel industry. Uncle Ken had met up with my Aunty in the war years when he was stationed at RAF Cosford. Like my own father, he had a northern accent. I think he too was in a protected trade but whilst in the RAF he was transferred to the Army and sent out to Singapore to fight the Japanese. Fortunately, they surrendered whilst he was

Before I Start

en route so his job was a peacekeeping role. He never really wanted to talk about the war years. I remember that their neighbour had been in a Japanese Prisoner Of War camp and had weals and lash marks across his back. Later in life, my Auntie proved to be a second mother (after my own had died) and was my biggest fan in my musical endeavours. My Aunty died in 2007. She was regal in old age and in death.

Once or twice a year my Aunty Joy would come to nans but she never seemed to be invited for dinner. She always appeared to invite herself and the adults were keen to despatch her on her way before she had hardly sat down. Neither my mom nor my Aunty Edith would ever talk about Aunty Joy. They were both protective of my nan and always seemed to unite in attendance at her house when Joy arrived. I was told that Aunty Joy had been "put away" in a mental institution from birth (Great Barr, Birmingham I believe). I never found out why but such occurences were not uncommon in those days. Unwanted children, out of wedlock children, orphaned children, disabled children were all "put away" somewhere. Aunty Joy looked more like my Aunty Edith than she did my mom and always appeared nervous in company. Neither my elder brother Keith nor my

Before I Start

cousin Roy were ever given the chance to bond with her. Apparently nan and Uncle Charlie would never sign her release papers. I have no idea why and my suspicions are best kept private. She remained in the institution all her life to my knowledge. She went on to become a carer at the hospital. I do not know if she is dead or alive.

My cousin Roy was my childhood playmate when opportunity presented itself. Usually this might be during school holidays or on Saturdays. He was one year younger than me so he and I enjoyed an affinity that he did not share with my elder brother Keith who was three years my senior. We would play all day long in nans verandah. Typically we would play at World War 2 soldiers, or cowboys and indians or marleys (marbles). We would weave our games around nan's tomato plants which would always bear a heavy crop and the smell of tomatoes always permeated the room. I was usually better at games than Roy but he was probably brighter than me and went on to teach at a senior level. I always felt there was a degree of competition between Roy and myself. This was never of our making, rather it was of our two mothers. Probably it was quite normal but nonetheless I think it put boundaries on our friendship.

Before I Start

I have two brothers, Keith and John. Keith was so named after my dads best friend. He was a brother and best friend through all of my growing up. At three years my senior he was always there to protect me as I tended to follow him through schools. Because of Keith, I was never bullied, never hurt and never picked on. By the time he had left Grammar School to go on to University, I was big enough to look after myself. Like him, I use words rather than fists. Probably moreso than him, I can use my fists effectively if I have to. Nonetheless, whilst I became a black belt in Karate, Keith was a Ju Jitsu student. Ju Jitsu was very popular post war. It had been taught in Her Majesty's Armed Forces and clubs opened up during the 1950's. I remember one boyhood tale of Keith being picked on by a group of other lads at a bus stop. He took them on single handed and beat them. I don't know how many there were. The number seemed to grow with the telling. Not his telling of course, he kept his own counsel, but clearly my mother had to tell everyone and a bit of creative licence probably crept in. Keith was the perfect elder brother. He was sent to bed when I set fire to the shed, he was charged to look after me and got into trouble if I was hurt in any way, I remember him as the one dragging a sceaming me through the lanes of Wheaton Aston when we were being

Before I Start

chased by a gang of lads on bikes back to our parents hardboard caravan. He was my guardian and never let me down. As is the case, as we grew into adulthood, the bond of childhood lessened. He went off to university and I was left at home. I never felt that my parents supported me in my university endevours as they did him. Perhaps they couldn't afford two at university, I don't know. Perhaps they couldn't bear two children away from home. Perhaps it suited me to think what I did, I don't know, its all a long time ago. Either way, I made it easy for them by not getting my grades and then falling out with them when I was subsequently offered a place and able to think of going. Keith was successful in his life. The continuous thread throughout his adulthood was education. He worked in a secondary school and a borstal. He was Headmaster of a private school and went on to teach in a University and a College of Further Education. Unlike me, he didn't enjoy a stable emotional or personal life but was eventually to meet his soulmate and finally enjoy a happy married life. It is strange how folk see each other. Keith probably sees me a making a big success of my life whilst I see him as equally if not more successful.

Before I Start

I have always felt very much a second born. There is a conception that the second born is emotionally deprived of the love that is poured on the first born. I quote (abridged) "The second born is the true perfectionist. This person attends to details and strives for perfection. Good enough is never good enough. Second borns are competitive. The second born competes with the first for parental attention. Emotions make life messy so second borns tend to ignore them. Second borns may not like compliments." (Barbara Pytel 2006).

Keith and I spent our childhood in a world of Carnation milk, commodes, Davenports beer at home, dipbread, Great Western Railways (GWR, known in Bilston as Low Level) , Hans and Lotte Hass, inkwells, London Midland Service (LMS, known in Bilston as High Level), mice, motorbikes and sidecars, National Savings Certificates, newts, nib pens, coal fired heating, outside lavatories , quartz radio, radiograms, smog, steam engines, sword dancing, tadpoles, transistors, trolley buses, wireless, policemen that smacked you round the "earole", teachers that caned you and parents that may repeat such punishment if you ever brought such shame on the family (and we say times were good)! Beyond us in the bigger world was the Commonwealth,

Before I Start

Communism, the jet engine and the race to the moon. Britain was still GREAT. World War 1 was the "Great War" and World War 2 was still an everyday talking point.

My younger brother, John is ten years my junior and because of that in many ways grew up as an only child. I was lucky because I had a role model in my elder brother that I could relate to but by the time John was ten, I was twenty. He may have thought I perceived him as a nuisance because of that. That was never the case and certainly when I met Jill, my wife to be, John's life was enriched in many ways with outings and holidays. By this time, my father , still working in the steel industry at George Gadd & Sons in Tipton, was also joint owner with my mother in a Post Office, Newsagents and sweet shop in Lower Street, Tettenhall. As children, Keith and I had grown up with walks out and vistis to Badger Dingle, Worfield and Claverley. In Bilston I recall walking the "cut" on a summers day with mom, dad, Keith and Bessie the dog (Bessie got into trouble for swimming in the "cut" having just been bathed). John seemed to have little of that and spent much time on his own. My mother loved him dearly but little input was put in by way of school or education whereas in my case, and Keiths, our

Before I Start

education was deemed to be crucial to our future. John could have easily fallen in with the wrong crowd and gone off the rails. It is testament to his own personality and strength of character that he never did. Keith and I look like my mom. John has all the traits of a Woodhead and carries forwards to future generations much of our late father. John has succeeded in his own life. A happy husband and father (a role in which he has excelled) he has the work ethic of our parents and been a dependable provider to his family. Mom was always proud of him. Dad would have been proud too.

Jill and I have brought two children into this world; two fine sons Simon and Ben. Simon excelled at school just like my brother Keith. He always preferred calculators and computers to toys and from a very early age demonstrated a love of business and self employment. After Grammar School he went on to become an Investment Adviser in the stock exchange industry. After that he went into business and had successes and failures. His greatest success has always been his own self belief and in many ways I see myself in him. I admire his single mindedness, his tenacity and his unswerving committment to succeed. I see all these traits more in him than myself as

Before I Start

mine are diluted with diversions such as the arts and music about which he appears to care not a jot. One day, perhaps he will write his own book but I doubt it. Perhaps in some way he may attribute some of his achievements in life to the upbringing given to him by his mom and myself.

Ben is my second son, some five years younger than his elder. Like me, he expresses many of the traits of a second sibling. Like me, Ben went to a grammar school that restrained rather than advanced his true abilities. Like me he is a musician. Ben lived more consciously through the time of my eccentricities. He resented being picked up from school in a donkey and cart never accepting that his friends thought it was "cool". In many ways, as a wage earner Ben has always been a round peg in a square hole, always struggled to find his vocation. Others could always see that he was a highly developed social being with a bottomless pit of ability to listen and care. A classic candidate for teaching or social service. Ben is himself a father, a role in which he excels. In my lifetime, he is the best father I have ever personally known. Like me, Ben may well write a book. His will be well worth reading.

Before I Start

My wife Jill and I met in the 1970's and in many ways are very different people. She is shy and retiring. Whilst I too am essentially an introvert, I compensate by outragous behaviour therefore appearing extrovert. She has never been one to steal the limelight, always one to enjoy seeing others achieve (even at her cost). She is a good person and one who has smoothed out my character excesses during our years together. She has supported and encouraged me throughout our married life. I have never known her to hold me back and has been there with me through everything I have attempted to do. She was adopted as a child and in some ways I guess that shows itself in her lack of roots and her subsequent need for stability and happiness in her domestic life. I know where I came from and what went before me. She has only ever known where she grew up. I cannot imagine my life story except as a link in a chain that started long before me and will continue long after. Her chain will continue too but she has never striven to find out where the chain began. She always feared such investigation may have offended her adopted parents and that may be true.

All these people have shared my life and in their own ways developed me as a human being and helped shape me into what I am.

Before I Start

In musical terms I must acknowledge :

1. St Leonard's Church, Bilston for a fine choral training
2. Ettingshall Primary School for the basics in song and dance
3. Vicky and George Evans and the Unicorn Folk Groups for introducing me to the world of entertaining.
4. Nigel Mazlyn Jones for being a friend and early guitar teacher.
5. The George Formby Society for friendship, stage skill and confidence building and its many members for friendship.
6. The several and varied bookers and agents who find me interesting and varied work.
7. Whoever it was all those hundreds of years ago that first came up with the idea of a One Man Band.
8. The many live musicians that inspire me as I go along.
9. MySpace for acting as a shopfront for the many performers who, just like me, make up the numbers in the hope of one day being "discovered".

I hope you enjoy my recollections.

(Gay) Pride & Prejudice

A hot summers night and there we were, parked in a layby on the A23, five miles north of Brighton, Jill my wife, and myself. The motorhome shook with a neverending stream of passing traffic. Although off the road, the lorries seemed almost on top of us. Thanks to a closure on the M1, it was now 12.30am and I had to report for duty by 10am next morning. We had been diverted off the M1 just north of Luton and had to pick our through and around Welywn Garden City following yellow "diversion" signs in the darkness. Still I was looking forward to seeing the statue of Max Miller.

The event was Brighton Pride 2007. I must confess to being slightly naive about homosexuality. I once worked with a bloke that had AIDS but he seemed as normal as me (hmmmm). I shared a bowl of chips with him one day in a London pub so it obviously didn't bother or give me grave cause for concern. I do remember his surprise. He was obviously used to reticence in such matters. He kept his condition as secret as possible. Such was the way before Princess Diana gave AIDS the seal of royal cognisance in 1987 when she sat on the bed of a sufferer and held his hand. She moved the whole world in that moment of contact.

(Gay) Pride & Prejudice

My only other experience with the "gay" community was in Wigan, Lancashire. I was working at Heinz at the time (the baked bean factory). I was not employed by Heinz but by one of their on site contractors. I was on site trying to resolve some staff and union issues. Discussions went on late into the night and when I walked out of the factory door, it was after 11.30pm. As the cold air hit my face, realisation that I had no hotel room booked suddenly dawned on me. I had to be back on shift at 6am next morning so sleep was a priority. I raced round to the hotel I usually stayed at, only to find the night security beginning to prepare the hotel for closure. He advised me that there were no rooms but pointed me in the direction of another hotel.

"Straight down the road and look for the roofline lit up by different coloured lights"

I found this hotel which in case it is still open will remain nameless. Reception was still open.

"Do you have a room please"
"Yes sir, single or double?"
"Whichever, it doesn't matter"
"How long would sir like to stay?"
"Just tonight please"
"All night?"

(Gay) Pride & Prejudice

"Yes, all night!"
I then duly signed in and awaited my key. No key was offered.
"May I have a key please"
"None of our rooms have keys"
"But surely, my things will not be safe if I leave the room"
" Your things are quite safe sir"

I found my room. Kilroy had been everywhere and under different circumstances there is no way I would have stayed. The lavatory seat was broken and on the floor, wallpaper was ripped and the bedside light stood at a strange angle with a dim yellow bulb.

I had still only been away from work some thirty minutes and I was still hyped up with the events of the day. I had dismissed someone which is never a pleasurable experience. I decided to have nightcap. I hid my posessions as best I could and crammed my pockets with anything portable and of value. Fortunately, this was the 1980's. Mobile 'phones and laptops were things of the future. I left my room and as I shut the door, noticed that the door handle was in the shape of what looked like a swans neck, long, slightly curved, firm to the touch and seemingly a perfect fit to the hand. "Strange" I thought.

(Gay) Pride & Prejudice

I descended the scruffy staircase with its raised flock wallpaper and unpleasantly stickily soiled carpet to find myself back at reception.

"Any chance of a nightcap please?"
"Yes sir, straight through the door, that way"
Through I went into a room that can only be described as brown. Brown curtains, brown velour settee. All in all a pretty depressing sight. A man was seated on a brown velour cushion on the brown velour settee.

"Excuse me mate, could you tell me where the bar is please"
"Straight through that door" he said.

I opened the door. Instantly my eyes were dazzled with the strobe of a bright flashing light. I instantly was dazzled and incapable of making much sense or where I was. I realised that the room was in darkness save for the strobe light. Like a lighthouse, as it lit, I had the briefest of momentary glimpses of my environment. I could make out very little except that it was some sort of dancefloor and some way in front of me was a table and some white plastic chairs, rather like you would have in the garden, complete with an umbrella.

(Gay) Pride & Prejudice

I made my way to it and as I did, realised that the room was some sort of night club and I was the only one on its dancefloor. As my eyes accustomed to the light, I picked out certain figures and realised that the bar was to my left and that I was walking away from it. I headed towards the bar, the light now behind me. As it strobed and as I got nearer to the bar, I realised an absence of females. Moreso, I realised that the bar staff were wearing leather waistcoats and caps with no shirts. Finally, the penny dropped, I realised I was in a gay hotel!

Switching to my best John Wayne swagger and preparing my deepest bass voice, I reached the bar and managed to order a scotch and ice. To be fair , no one approached me but I nonetheless beat a hasty retreat back to the brown velour room. I edged my way through the door (backwards as I recall) and dropped into what was now a safe and inviting velour cushion. As I did, I am sure a cloud of dust burst forth, hanging like a cloud around me.

"This is a gay hotel I retorted with a surprised tone to the man sat nearby"
"I know he said " in his best Kenneth Williams drawl. "I always stay here".

(Gay) Pride & Prejudice

Realising I was in a predicament, I thought it best to act naturally, as though I was used to this sort of thing and then exit his company without fuss or fear. It turned out that he was a sheet music salesman who in the late 1980's was still what could be called a Commercial Traveller. He had no company car but travelled everywhere by bus and train, presumably staying in gay hotels!

I jammed the door that night with a chair. My dreams were somewhat intimate and personal though not in a way that pleasured me. I slept well enough in spite of my unusual circumstances.

The next day I was out by 5.30am but liking my value for money, was back for breakfast at 7.30am. The "restaurant" (I use the title loosely), was crammed with road workers or "navvys" as we used to call them. I couldn't believe they were all staying at a gay hotel and still wonder as to their reasoning. I saw my sheet music salesman in the company of a navvy and guessed he had made a "friend".

Naiively, I told my new workmates where I had stayed. They seemed to keep their distance and I am sure that the lavatory emptied when I went in! Clearly a rumour went around the factory. Apparently the

(Gay) Pride & Prejudice

hotel owner was in prison for committing an indecent act on the dancefloor. This is only heresay but it's truth would not surprise me!

Some months later, my wife and family were heading north from Bridlington and came upon Whitley Bay. We had been trying to find Newcastle Upon Tyne but seemed to be directed anywhere but. We seemed to go round it, if not over it, but never into it. Whitley Bay I had never visited but understood it to be a sort of North Eastern Blackpool. Such a place would surely be crammed with hotels and Guest Houses. We had two kids and a Great Dane in the car and were needing to find a bed for the night. In the distance we saw a roofline illuminated by coloured lights. We stopped, told the dog to look after the kids and went in to reception.

"Good evening. Do you have a room please?"
"How long for sir?"
"Just tonight please"
"Will that be all night sir?"

We were gone!

My only other exposure to homosexuality, at that time, was again staying at another gay hotel. This time it was in Blackpool. It is still

(Gay) Pride & Prejudice

there to this day. My wife and I were up there for a George Formby Convention. The hotel was superb, the hospitality second to none. It was spotlessly clean and every attention to service was met in flawless detail. The hosts, whilst clearly of that persuasion, were otherwise as normal as their hetrosexual guests. I guess it was not a gay hotel. Rather it was a hotel owned and managed by a gay couple.

The Brighton gig came as a result of a London marketing company booking me for a street carnival in the "south east". The south east turned out to be Brighton. The carnival – Pride 2007, claimed to be Europe's largest gathering of gay men, lesbians, transexuals, cross dressers and indeed other sexual denominations about which I knew nothing and still know precious little.

It was with some trepidation that I put the bed up in the motorhome that night. Of greatest concern was the fact that the parade had a "musical" theme and I had been booked by a corporate sponsor to work with a troupe of Mary Poppins dancers, professional West End dancers. Now, Mary Poppins isn't exactly One Man Band stuff; it's a bit too complicated. As a One Man Band, I have always performed my own songs or carefully selected ditties that have a

(Gay) Pride & Prejudice

good thumping rhythm. Waltzes and variable tempo stuff is not the chosen style of this One Man Band. I would have to practically sprint with the tempo of "Supercali....", lope to "Let's Go Fly A Kite", bounce to "Chim Chiminee" and march to "Spoonful of Sugar". One Man Band busking is usually about a 30 second audience. In that short moment of time you have to sell yourself and tell the story. If you succeed the audience stays and becomes a songs length or even two. Usually, as a One Man Band, I am stationary and my job is to "arrest" the passer by. In this case, the audience was to be stationary and I was on parade. As such, the audience was truly a 30 second one at most before I would be out of earshot. Mary Poppins songs were not of a 30 second construction!

I had a Scotch in bed, tried to remember the lyrics & forget what lay ahead the next day. The motorhome rocked throughout the night as each articulated lorry whooshed by. It was as though we were surfers riding the wave.

Every hour ticked relentlessly on. My mind was too active for sleep and the continous stream of traffic reminded me at time second intervals not to dare to nod! As it was I sneaked a few heavily interrupted hours and

(Gay) Pride & Prejudice

woke blearily at 7.30am on Saturday, August 4th – the day of PRIDE 2007, the day of the march, the day I knew so little of!

After a hasty and brief breakfast I telephoned Chris, my contact from the Agency. I had to be at his house by 10am. The arrangement was that he would take us to a meeting point then accompany my wife and the motorhome to the "terminus" of the parade so that when over, I could easily pile all my kit and myself into an easily accessible refuge!

I was concerned that I used the lavatory twice more than is normal in a morning and was worried how I would cope with any toiletry needs en route! I claim never to get nerves before a gig but that isn't entirely true. If there is anything new about the gig, I do get nervous and concern myself, needlessly, with all the things that may go wrong. Such concern usually manifests itself in frequent visits to the loo. The result is a sore bum. I didn't need a sore bum today, not with a two mile hike in front of me (on the hottest day so far). My piles worried me too. Anyway, I didn't want a sore bum in Brighton for lots of reasons. I decided to apply a little Vaseline and felt instantly more relaxed. I couldn't imagine having to go to

(Gay) Pride & Prejudice

my doctor and explain that I had got a sore bum in Brighton.

Without the aid of SATNAV (because I hadn't yet bought one), we easily found his house and waited nearby for his arrival. Eventually he turned up. An amiable sort of chap, he was one of the many who choose to live away from London and partake of the daily commute. Two hours added to the working day always seemed an odd choice of working life to me. However, in the promise of the Brighton day, I could well see why he chose to live here. The place looked clean and tidy and there was certainly a buzz, even here on the outskirts. I hadn't realised before I arrived at Brighton that it was a city. Not the city of Brighton, but rather of Brighton & Hove. I later learned that the Hove population perhaps felt a little consumed by Brighton and perhaps had some sort of resistance movement fighting the Hove corner. I late saw a sign that read "This is not Brighton City it is the City of Brighton <u>And Hove</u>". The underlining said it all. Hove was not going to lose out!

In many ways it is a sad thing when populations are consumed . I remember being a proud Bilstonian when a lad. Later, in 1966, we were "absorbed" into Wolverhampton and became little more than

(Gay) Pride & Prejudice

a district. We lost a vibrant town centre, a Town Hall, even the railway station eventually went, all because Wolverhampton sucked every resource out of the area. To this day, proud Bilstonians still fight for their towns identity. Bilston was mentioned in the Doomsday book but was digested by Wolverhampton during the swinging sixties. England might have won the world cup in football, but that same year marked the end of Bilstons sense of identity.

Places like Warrington, famous for that Lancashire lad, George Formby are now in Cheshire but many Warringtonians still think of themselves as Lancastrians. Many resent being in Cheshire. Many of the old county names have gone too. I loved living in Salop but have far less pleasure living in Shropshire and it takes up more room on a letter! "Salop" oozed heritage. "Shropshire" says nothing. Names matter to people but the system cares not a jot for thee and me. Progress demands change and we suffer! I guess I could share many hours of moaning with some of the residents of Hove!

Anyway, back to the gig. Chris (my contact), directed us as near to the parade start as was possible. I was amazed at the crowds. Thousands of people lined the streets & we were lucky to get high above the seafront

(Gay) Pride & Prejudice

from where I could descend by foot to the rendezvous. Chris was then to drive the motorhome and my wife, back to Preston Park, where the parade would end. He had arranged to leave me on the steps near Sea World where I was to wait for my escort & sponsor. It was 10am. The sun was hot and I was in top hat and tails with a drum on my back , morris dancers bells on my bare legs, shorts and a banjolele. I had chosen to leave the 12 string guitar thinking the banjo sound would carry better in open air. Another first,

(Gay) Pride & Prejudice

I had never used the banjo in a One Man Band setting before!

Waiting on the steps I became a focus of attention, repeatedly photographed by people from foreign lands who obviously thought me an eccentric Englishman (which I guess I am, slightly). It's strange how other people see you. I have been told so often that I am eccentric yet I don't see myself in that way. It seems very normal to me to wear a deerstalker hat, drive a pair of donkeys and earn my living as a one man band singing silly songs with zero commercial value. Add to that my wife and I owning a commercial laundry and I think that makes us pretty average "Joes".

One bloke, who I think came from Scandinavia, (he was so white as to only be from a cold country and his command of English was very Germanic. He was however very friendly, never mentioned the war and asked me if I liked ABBA), photographed me several times and kept starting conversations and touching bits of my apparatus. I couldn't help but hide behind my English reticence as I was unused to such attention except from passing dogs. (I remember busking once when a dog used my spare guitar, stood on it's stand, as a lampost! I thought this Scandinavian bloke

(Gay) Pride & Prejudice

might be after my body which whilst a new experience, seemed highly inappropraite given the circumstances, the public location and my age. At 58, I no longer considered myself an object of sexual interest. With white hair and a white beard, whilst I am still 21 in my head, I recognize that my thinning scalp and growing paunch render me insignificant to the vast female populous. Except that is when entertaining the elderly, which I do a lot.

Now to a lady of 99 years of age, a man in his late 50's is but a boy and I have had my fair share of admirers in the 80 plus age group. Older ladies seem to lose their inhibitions. They think nothing of touching and feeling and can be openly promiscuous. I think, with my limited knowledge, that this somehow is a result of dementia or perhaps Alzheimers. In that I hold this view, you will appreciate that such elderly attentions do not fuel my sexual awareness. I guess in someway it is a backhanded compliment.

My new Scandinavian friend was perhaps just being friendly. I hadn't adjusted yet to the hedonistic environment of Brighton & Hove nor it's pleasure seeking population so I was naturally guarded. Anyway, I came from Salop (sorry Shropshire). Exposure to such personal, scrutinous and perhaps

(Gay) Pride & Prejudice

intimate attention is unusual in Ironbridge, Bridgnorth or Shrewsbury.

I don't really know how I came to get this gig, I am not local to Brighton, more the Midlands and Wales. In fact I hadn't been to Brighton for years. The last time I had been was for a Healthcare conference when I did a proper job. I remember going to a pub with a friend from London. I knew Brighton was different when I went to the lavatory. Most " Gents" have bare walls (apart from Kilroy & other graffiti). Upmarket facilities may have pictures of a village cricket match on the green, amusing fishermans pictures (if you are near water – fishing water that is), steam engines (if near a railway) or other male related pursuits – cars, engineering even women. Not the lavatory in the pub in Brighton. This had a big sign which said "Lubricating jelly available from bar". Thankfully no one came in the loo whilst I was there otherwise I think I may have disgraced myself – and it was summer!

Gentlemen (of my generation) will allow ourselves to be dressed by our wives. Whilst we would be quite happy to choose a dark colour, usually the same one that we have chosen before, our wives insist on beige or similar light coloured trousers as soon as the sun shines. They fail to understand that such

(Gay) Pride & Prejudice

a colour is no good in the Gents! Especially no good when nervously handling one's privates in a pub in Brigton which offers lubricating jelly. I have seen many a man discreetly drying his trousers under a Warner Howard dryer. They were always the best. A good jet of hot air. None of this low voltage stuff, bought on the cheap and capable of drying nothing – hands included.

The slightest flick of one's privates can result in a long dark dribble down a lightly coloured leg. How do you walk back through the pub with an obviously stained leg? If the lavatory has a roller towel or paper, you are quite literally buggered, (well perhaps not exactly "buggered", not as it might be understood in Brighton). Frantic rubbing with a paper towel to generate heat and so neutralise the offending stain can lead to a dye transfer of blue or green if the towel is coloured (so I am told). Cabinet roll towels were of course never desgned to dry one's lower regions, Great on the face or hand, preferrred in fact, but absolutely useless in a case of genital dribble.

I have often wondered as I have grown older quite why men are designed the way they are. It is quite obvious that without a cap at the end, any tube will leak. A penis after all, is but a biological tube. Strange that such an

(Gay) Pride & Prejudice

item should serve both waste discharge and sexual penetration purpose. Obvious to most of us therefore why AIDS got a grip! Simple case of cross contamination! Perhaps if I was an inventor, I might come up with some sort of penile glove. Something waterproof that a man could drop his Percy into.

Naming one's genital extension Percy, or Peter or the many other names we men give our penis is a strange thing to do. I wonder if women have a name for their bits and pieces? Mary or Doris seems hardly fitting but then neither is Lulu or Lucy.

Anyway, back to the gig. I had done a programme called "The Busker Symphony" for Channel 4 TV. This was broadcast in April 2007 having been shot and recorded in London during August, 2006. Then there was my web site "woodysonemanband.co.uk". There were links on the web page to Channel 4 and to "The Busker Symphony" and of course this is the age of GOOGLE. This search engine amazes me. I routinely communicate with other like minded individuals, one man bands that is. We find each other via GOOGLE or YAHOO or ASK JEEVES! Gone are the barriers of time zones, frontiers, mountains or coastlines. We can talk to people in China or Tibet. The internet has

(Gay) Pride & Prejudice

translation facilities ! (I know this because I started life as a technical translator. I was an early casualty of the computer age).

Computers when I was young filled a room or even a building. I entered the workplace with BRUNSVIGA's (mechanical adding machines). You could always tell the old hands in the office because they could make music as they whizzed the handle arround to multiply one number by another. Then of course there were COMPTOMETERS, at least I think that's what they were. An elite sub section of highly trained ladies would operate these typewriter like instruments. I never really worked out what they did. I don't understand computers so a Comptometer is still beyond my ability to explain. Interesting that they were operated by ladies in a ladies typing pool. These of course were the days when men did mens work and women did womens. I don't recall any malefolk in the typing pool. I do recall that women who broke free of their "station" and rose to supervisory or management roles in male dominated job areas, were viewed with some suspicion by the menfolk and were always objects of sexual fantasy, usually the men were going to "teach them something"! Sounds very out of place now, almost an arrestable offence, but then things were different, not better, just diferent.

(Gay) Pride & Prejudice

I don't remember any homosexuals in my youth, except perhaps the English teacher. He took far too much pleasure from slippering a boys bare bottom in an all boys school. Even so, my mother trusted me to go on holiday with him (and three other boys). To be fair he never approached me in any sexual way. I don't know if he approached anyone else either but friend Chris was known as a real lad (where girls were concerned anyway). Blonde Tommy Steele hair and winklepicker shoes made him the focus of them all, that is until he was arrested. A neighbour, looking through the bedroom window saw him acting inapproriately with his pet Alsation dog. The police took him away and the dog was seized by the RSPCA or was it the PDSA? Can't remember. Most girls went off him then. Oddly, some increased their pursuit of him so "having a dog" must be attractive to certain girls? Perhaps the fact that he had "done it", even with a dog, somehow made him more mature.

We never used the word gay in those days, the 1950's and '60's. Well certainly not in suburbia. Perhaps they did in London, I don't know. If we had, every George Formby song, and I think there were about 240, would have had a homosexual

(Gay) Pride & Prejudice

reference! When George sang about gayness he was singing about things joyous and happy. I think the first time I remember "gay" being redefined was in the days of Larry Grayson. He had wonderful catch phrases, completely unfunny except that he was a master of delivery. He could have made me laugh reading a menu. There is nothing funny about saying "Shut that door" but with a Larry Grayson glance, a flick of the head and a purse of the lips, the nation was his slave and quite rightly so.

"Oh what a gay day" Larry would say. He was very feminine in his delivery and I recall understanding a double entendre in his use of the word "gay". I never remember it before Larry. So, perhaps gay men owe their naming to Larry.

Larry Grayson was well known as a friend of Noele Gordon, the hotel proprietress (Meg Richardson) of Crossroads. Crossroads was the Midlands response to Coronation Street. Initially produced by Associated Television (ATV), latterly it was produced by Central. It was known for its dodgy sets and poor acting which in my view was always unfair. The character of Benny, played by Paul Henry, has probably only ever been equalled by David Lonsdale who plays David Stockwell in Heartbeat.

(Gay) Pride & Prejudice

Larry Grayson, came to fame in his 50's. Before then he had been deemed too camp for TV. He made two appearances in Crossroads but was best known for his role as game show host in The Generation Game and Shut That Door. His catch phrases of "seems like a nice boy" and "just look at the muck in here" together with his stories about the make believe characters of Everard, Slack Alice, Apricot Lil, Pop It In Pete and Self Raising Fred paved the way for those to follow. He had a gentle humour and an inoffensive delivery.

Being gay sounds so much more fun that being homosexual, homo or queer and certainly the latter two were the words of my day. Not that I ever used them because I honestly do not remember seeing or knowing any (except the aforementioned teacher). Even he was not in any way effeminate. He was rather brutal and with the benefit of what I know now I can imagine him being the male contributor to any relationship and being rather rough with it (reciting poetry at the same time of course).

Oddly enough, I remember studying for my A level English. Certain books were compulsory such as The Tempest by Willian

(Gay) Pride & Prejudice

Shakespeare and Edward the Second by Phillip Marlow I think. Hated both of those but I did love The Grapes of Wrath by Richard Steinbeck and have only recently revisited it as an adult. I now know that it fits perfectly with my love of Woody Guthrie and Jimmie Rodgers, but I didn't know that at the time.

We had free choice of one book to study, free choice that is except that it had to be selected from a list of choices. The whole class chose Macbeth. I chose "Sons and Lovers" by DH Lawrence. The English teacher tried all he could to persuade and cudjole me into joining the rest of the class. He even called my parents to school and told me that my choice meant he was unable to help me and I would have to study it on my own. Thinking back, perhaps Lawrence made him feel uncomfortable (just like me in Brighton). Anyway I studied Lawrence on my own and read most of his books. I still love Lawrence today both books and poems. I think Lawrence scraped me through my A level English. Certainly the English teacher expressed huge admiration for my empathy and understanding of the text. Perhaps in my choice I was already sowing the seeds of going it alone, just like now as a One Man Band.

(Gay) Pride & Prejudice

Just reflecting on the changing use of words. Let me take you back to 1756 when someone wrote: *"Lavender blue, dilly dilly, lavender green"*.

It was a really dirty song in its day. "Dilly dilly" had a certain sexual meaning describing the first sexual exploration of young woman by young man and promising marriage if he was allowed to "dilly dilly"! One hundred years later the song reappeared, pretty much as originally written, still using the words "dilly dilly", but now it was a nursery rhyme for children. Like the word gay, the meaning of dilly dilly had changed completely. I doubt anyone would say today that they had had a gay time without understanding the expected interpretaion of such a remark.

Where was I, Oh yes, "The Busker Symphony". It was written and directed by Benjamin Till and broadcast in 4 parts on Channel 4 TV in April 2007. The timing was awful. Coronation Street was on Channel 3, ITV, and it was the conclusion of the trial of Tracy Barlow who as I am sure you will remember had killed her builder boyfriend, Charlie. The whole world was watching Tracy's trial and it was my TV debut.

Actually, I wrote a song accompanied by my ukulele.:

(Gay) Pride & Prejudice

"Is she guilty or is she not, Tracy Barlow the Street's harlot
April 2nd, the day of the trial and all my fans are in denial
'Cos Woody's debut is on TV
But Tracy's trial is on Channel 3

So who'll get the viewers who'll do the best
Tracy's trial or Woody's quest
Who'll make the headline, be the viewers choice
Tracy's lies or Woody's voice
I phoned all my friends and I told them the news
I'm on Channel 4 before the news

They sounded pleased but I knew they were lying
They were more concerned with Charlie's dying
Then it came, the day in my life
I sat at the telly, just me and the wife
Then she said without a smile
I didn't know you clashed with Tracy's trial

Now it's over, it's all behind me
Tracy's a star & I'm history
I search every day for my fan mail
But she gets more and she's in jail

It came and went like a clap of thunder
Woody's OMB, the Three Minute Wonder
But I made the news for all to see
The Telford Journal, page thirty three".

To be true to events, it wasn't the Telford Journal, it was the Shropshire Star. Nor was it page thirty three, but that rhymes better.

(Gay) Pride & Prejudice

The Busker Symphony, in four parts, was broadcast over four nights, Apirl 2nd being the first. My part was the first and was called ANDANTE. It featured *"Woodys One Man Band and the Sounds of the Streets of London"*. What I learned when working with Benjamin and Julia, (the producer), was that this was a small world that I had been invited into. A classic example of who you know not what!

Filming on Sclater Street in London E1 was quite an experience for someone like me, from the sticks. Occasional passers by would recognise some of our crew especially Julia. "Not seen you since Cannes" one remarked. "Are you going to Edinburgh?" asked another.

Julia had selected Sclater Street for it's murals. I realised the craft of these people. You or I could walk this street any day and never see it in the way a film maker can. She and Ben saw opportunity in street debris, rubbish, manhole covers, street noise, shop items, brickwork, street art. The finished product turned out to be an exquisite testimonial to their two crafts and those of their crew.

(Gay) Pride & Prejudice

Following on from ANDANTE, I had received some tentative enquires from a few terrestial and satellite TV stations. What I had also learned was that most came to nothing so I had ceased to get excited anymore about the "big break". The Brighton gig was one such similar enquiry. To me as a proud Salopian, an enquiry from a London agency was bound to result in nothing. I had been approached to perform in Covent Garden, St David's Hall Cardiff and on a couple of well known TV programmes. Most came to nothing. As such I simply mailed off an eMail reply when the enquiry came through –
"Yes I was free"
"No I wouldn't play all day – 90 minutes maximum"
"By the way I would like a meal allowance of £25"
"No I wasn't free of charge, I had to earn a living, £300 plus expenses".

The contract came through and here I now stood on the sea front dripping with sweat looking rather out of place in this cosmo-sexual-politan world, dressed in a top hat and tails (on the hottest day of the year), with a big drum on my back etc etc

Just in front of me on the steps were two very muscular males. They were holding

(Gay) Pride & Prejudice

hands. Both looked like bodybuilders. You certainly wouldn't have picked a fight with them yet there they were openly and physically proclaiming their devotion to each other. By that I mean, they were unafraid to show their affection. They were kissing and squeezing and holding each other. Not in any sexual way, Rather it was a demonstration of fondness, affection, even love. They wore rather unusual trousers in that there were no "backsides" in them. You could see their bottoms! Fine, well honed bottoms they were too. A modesty strip disappeared between their buttocks but that was it. Now I don't know about you but I have piles. I would worry that my personal problems would be there for the world to see.

I wonder if gay men have piles? It would be terribly inconvenient if you see what I mean! I don't know if gay men do have piles. If they don't then perhaps it might be all the lubricating jelly that the pubs sell! The first thing any of us does with piles is to buy a lubricant. ANUSOL! I wonder what marketing wizz kid came up with that name. He or she clearly never imagined standing in a queue in Boots on a Saturday :

"May I have a tube of ANUSOL please?"

(Gay) Pride & Prejudice

"Sorry sir, I can't hear you" says the attractive 18 year old female student.
"May I have some ANUSOL please, cream for my anal disorder"
"Sorry sir, I can't hear you, Please speak up"
"HAVE YOU ANY CREAM FOR MY PILES?"
"No need to shout sir, I'm only here to help"

Where was I? Two gay men in bottomless trousers. These were men that would turn any womans head, Well honed, well dressed (except for bare bottoms), as the saying goes, "tall, dark & handsome". In fact, I wouldn't be exaggerating if I described them as overtly male . Yet, they were gay!

Just in front of them were two women - stereotypically lesbian, as though they had crafted their appearance from an instruction book. Baggy trousers to hide their female contours, bracers, short hair, big boots. (Is it bracers or braces? English and American is so intertwined today. To me "braces" is a woodworking or dentistry term. My dad wore bracers!) "Bovver" girls you could have called these two. Again they were openly "familiar" and particularly hostile to anyone else, or so I thought. In fact during the time I saw them, they only had eyes for each other, as though they had just met. They seemed to exude a deep committment

(Gay) Pride & Prejudice

and an uncompromising love for each other without any reference to sex. Strange as a man, I have always struggled with understanding male homosexuality but never with female lesbiansim. I suppose in that I find women attractive so I can understand why they do too!

I felt quite out of place and very "rural". Just then an overtly gay man sidled along the seafront with a megaphone. "Cheer, you bitches" was his cry. Well I certainly didn't respond to being called a bitch. Other people might cheer but I needed to be asked properly – with courtesy and a more gentle form of language! Just hearing such a word actually made me feel uncomfortable and I was embarrassed at my own discomfort.

My eyes began to adjust to the scene before me. I became aware that some "women" were not women at all but rather attractive men! I also noted the number of "normal" folk, openly enjoying their day in the midst of this strange company of people who were clearly diiferent to them and to me. Then there was the contrast between the gentility and uncontroversial behaviour of the two lesbian women and the two gay men, and the open and very vocal haranging by our nominated, "course cheerleader". This was confusing.

(Gay) Pride & Prejudice

Just then my mobile rang :
"Woody?"
"Yes, I replied.
"Where are you?"
"Well I'm stood on the steps by Sea World on the promenade".
"How will we recognise you?"
"Well I'm wearing top hat and tails with a big red drum on my back"
"What can you see in front of you"
"The sea, oh and a gas lamp" (I hadn't realised that the whole sea front was lined with lamps, hundreds of them, all fashioned on the old gas lights).
"Anything else?"
"Well there's two lesbians and two male bodybuilders with no arse in their trousers!"
"That doesn't help. There's thousands here!"
"Well I can see the sign for Sea World on my right"
"Ok, you get there and I will come and meet you"

Now such an instruction might be ok if you're travelling light. I wasn't. About 30lbs of kit plus winter dress did not assist my passage through hundreds of people, to get to the prescribed location. Furthermore I was hardly nondescript. Every time I moved, bells rang and tambourines rattled. Of course a frontal view was of an unusually

(Gay) Pride & Prejudice

dressed crackpot. What few could see was what came behind ie a big bass drum.

Eventually I did get there. I seemed to be surrounded by persons of questionable gender and found myself staring at the ground rather than engaging people's gaze. I certainly solicited no interest and was genuinly afraid of smiling in case I conveyed the wrong message. Furthermore, my knees were exposed – I felt very vulnerable and strangely out of place! I guess most men are not built for shorts and like most men of my age, mine were not the pinnacle of current fashion. They weren't exactly Army Surplus but they were khaki cotton and in these days of three quarter shorts, were unfashionably short in length. I guess they looked like boy scout shorts.

Now there is nothing wrong with boy scout shorts, if you are a boy scout. I should also add that in Salop, these shorts were pretty much par for the course but here I was in a big and very unusually liberated city. I did feel old fashioned, outdated square and morally naive. My shorts said all this in one glance!

Just then I heard "Woody, Woody" and this bulky but sprightly 30 something years old chap was gesticulating in my direction.

(Gay) Pride & Prejudice

"Over here, over here". That was easy for him to say but there was a crowd control fence between us and no way could I vault it. Inching my way along, as I learned later, in the opposite direction to that we were eventually to go, I finally found it's conclusion and joined him in the road.

"You're in the wrong place" he cried, clearly fraught with organisational stress. "We are further up the promenade". As it turned out, this was back in the direction I had travelled from. "The parade is due to start, We must hurry".

Now when I designed my One Man Band, I had standing in one place in mind, perhaps the odd shuffle. I never envisaged sprinting several hundred yards up a busy road cluttered with folk, very friendly folk, tactile folk, you know, the touchy feely kind. They seemed to block my every endeavour and were keen to talk and photograph me. At one point a large American "lady" physically apprehended me and insisted in a photoshoot with "this Englishman". My sponsor, clearly irate, reminded me that I was "his" for the day and not to be waylaid. He looked like a nice bloke but what being "his" meant caused me some concern as did the use of the word "laid". For a big man he was light on the loafers and would

(Gay) Pride & Prejudice

certainly beat me in a race. I later guessed that he was the dancers teacher and of course was thus exceptionally fit, in spite of his size!

Anyway, here I am running up the road with a bass drum beating relentlessly on my back, morris bells bouncing on my legs and a banjolele slipping from my sweaty grip.
What I haven't mentioned is my new development. This was a lyric holder or rather a collapsed music stand, strapped with electric ties to the inside of my drum. It poked out the front and had secured to it, thanks to bulldog clips, the lyrics to the four songs I had to sing. I had only had a few days to learn them and as they were not in my Top 10, I feared that I would forget the words , hence the prompt cards. As I ran, my lyric holder bounced around and I feared for it's longevity.

I became aware of the hugeness of this event. Dozens and dozens (many dozens that is) of heavy goods vehicles all decorated and themed to particular musicals. Other displays, like ours were on foot but again were clearly the result of hours of painstaking work and attention to detail.

Eventually, I saw Mary Poppins and her troupe – a gang of half a dozen chimney

(Gay) Pride & Prejudice

sweeps! I must confess to being thrilled at their costume authenticity and I hadn't seen them dance yet! As it turned out they were superb dancers and had the crowds enthralled. They were either fascinated or amused to see me and an impromptu rendering of "You Are My Sunshine" broke the ice and caused a giggle. I was relieved to arrive, delighted that my lyric stand had survived the test and impressed that my many hours of garage modifications to my One Man Band rig, had passed with flying colours, a test that I had never forseen ie a 2/300 yard sprint.

Obviously, as a One Man Band, I have done a number of street parades, carnivals, fairs, festivals. It never ceases to amaze me that my rig seems to survive whatever is demanded of it. It securing terms it comprises, luggage straps, electrical ties and elastic bands. That is pretty much it. It has never let me down and no part of it has ever failed – yet!

(Gay) Pride & Prejudice

So anyway, there we were finally together. Woody's One Man Band and the Mary Poppins Dancers, sponsored by a new mobile phone retailer in the Brighton area of Brighton and Hove.

Early Musical Beginnings

"I once had dreams and schemes and themes for life"
Paul Woodhead, September 2nd, 2007

Born in 1949, I grew up listening to the sounds of the 1950's and 60's. I had my first kiss to "She Loves You" by the Beatles. Christine was her name and I was in my mid teens. We were huddled against a wall on a cold winters night in Bilston, after church one Sunday evening. Church was great for picking up the girls especially as I was Head Chorister. That meant that I wore a large badge of office around my neck on a thick royal blue ribbon. As Head Choirboy, I had sung on the TV and on the BBC Light Programme as it was then called. I had also sung at Lichfield Cathedral. I and three other choristers had been the visual on the front of St Leonard's Christmas card. This made me quite a catch in the little world of St Leonard's in Bilston. Absolutely irrelevant anywhere else, but in Bilston I was Head Chorister in the town's main church.

I remember Bilston as a proud town. A town with history traceable right back through time. A town that had links via St Leonards into deepest Africa. In fact we had a curate out there. Every Sunday, I would be glued to the notice board to see

Early Musical Beginnings

the latest pictures from Africa, the stories, the characters. Bilston had a vibrant feel.

Sunday night meant all the girls would sit upstairs staring down at us lads in the choir and did we love it! Those were the days when a church packed them in. Downstairs would be full every Sunday, morning and evening or Matins and Evensong to give them their proper names. Regular worshippers were so regular that they had their own seats, not officially reserved, but no one else dared ever to sit in them. Visitors seemed to know that certain seats were out of bounds and would look despairingly until a layperson escorted them to a free seat. I was a devout believer in those days as were all my friends. Unquestioning belief was drummed into me at every opportunity. The idea of impropriety with our young lady friends never entered our heads, well it entered, but never got any further. Sex education hadn't been invented and the "Birds and the Bees" were supposedly an adult secret until just prior to marriage at which point dad would talk to son or mum to daughter.

All of us, both girls and boys had grown up in the 1950's. We were the late baby boomers ie products of the population

Early Musical Beginnings

explosion post World War 2. The early baby boomers were 1945 to 1947 as the war with Germany and Japan ended. Troops continued post war in a beseiged Berlin and elswhere. Most of us were the second child following the immediate post war rush. We had been brought up in a non materialistic world. I remember my gran having her first fridge. It may have been the first in Bilston. It was certainly the first in my life. Most families still used a marble slab in the "larder". Most houses had a larder or a cupboard called a larder where the marble slab was kept. Being marble it was naturally cold so would offer some longevity to perishable goods. That being said, this was the nation pre supermarkets so shopping was still done daily or certainly every other day. Shops were what we would now call "specialist" – butchers, bakers, provisions, hardware etc.

Bilston boasted a full array of every imaginable shop and then had one of the best retail markets as well. Cotterills sold toys, Snapes sold drapery, Mason's sold what we would now call delicatessen items, Hartills sold electrical goods. People came for miles to shop in Bilston. Added to that, mobile deliveries were still very popular. I well remember the milkman (horse drawn

Early Musical Beginnings

of course), the pop man and the greengrocer. In those days, the milkman sold milk (and orange juice), the pop man sold pop, the greengrocer sold fruit and veg. It might sound blatantly obvious, but this was the era when demand was still met by specialists. The pop man didn't need to sell anything other than pop. He could make a good living at selling pop. Fizzy drinks (pops) were usually locally produced brands. This was a world pre a Cola dominated market. Buying was done on the street and on the doorstep.

Other street vendors included the rag and bone man. Again, horse drawn, he was a well regarded member of society. Not viewed with suspicion as today's "tatters" are, this was an early pioneer of the green world we now strive to achieve. The rag 'n bone man would take anything, usually in exchange for a sticky lolly for the kids. Somehow, he found a paying market for everything. Nothing went to waste, everything had a value. His horse would stand quietly in the street grazing from a leather bag of feed hanging from it's head. At it's other end, droppings would land on "th'ossroad" with a smelly, hot plop. These would end up on the garden or allotment. I usually had the job of clearing them up.

Early Musical Beginnings

My nan's rhubarb would win any prize thanks to the fruit and veg man's horse.

There was little traffic of course. Most people still used the bus , bicycle or shank's pony (feet) to get from A to B. People generally didn't travel very far. Life was local or at most a bus journey away. Buses of course were trolley buses ie they ran from electricity in overhead power lines to which they were connected by poles. "Poles cum off miss" was an excuse that no teacher could argue with when late. It was impossible to question and anyway, we had been taught not to tell lies so why would she ask us? When the poles came off, the conducter would evacuate everyone from the bus. He would then extract a long pole which ran in a tube underneath the nearside of the bus. The pole had a hook at the end and the bus poles had a receiver into which he would hook his pole and then try to reconnect to the overhead wires.

Early Musical Beginnings

There was usually much flashing and I guess this was why we were evacuated. We were no colder of course outside than we were on the bus. The bus had a large platform open on two sides to whatever elements there were on the day. There was no heating except upstairs where smoking was allowed. The upstairs ceiling always seemed to condense with syrupy droplets. I guess they were drops of water suspended nicotine. People bathed at most once a week and deoderants were to my knowledge not yet in use; we certainly had none. Most days the inside windows were dripping with brown condensation which I would clean off with my jacket sleeve. The best seat upstairs was at the front, right above the drivers seat. Downstairs, the bus had it's alighting and leaving landing which lead to two bench seats and then as upstairs indivual two person benches. The landing had a collector for used tickets and I remember that most people used it. On the landing was a luggage area for suitcases etc. The conducter also had a special area for his silver metal box which I guess contained additional rolls of tickets. Trolley buses ran at around 15mph I believe and in Bilston were two tone green and cream! Every child wanted to be a bus driver or better still a conductor. Conductors had the

Early Musical Beginnings

little ticket machine with a push lever and they had a leather money bag. Trolley buses were double decked with chromium metalwork that never rusted as it was continously polished by hundreds of hands every day. I do remember one "female" conductor. She had short hair and always wore trousers just like the men. I guess she may have been lesbian but I didn't know that then. Other than her, female conductors always looked like women though they usually did wear trousers because of going upstairs. The staircase to the upper deck did a ninety degree turn half way up. At this point it had a round mirror looking at the upper decking. This was so that when the conductor was downstairs, he/she could see what was going on upstairs. As schoolboys, we learned that if you sat on the inside, nearside, lower deck bench seat, the mirror gave a view up a girls skirt if she went to the upper deck. Such was the limit of 1950's voyeurism.

Back to street retailing. At the high tech end was the laundryman. He would drive a motor van. Laundries were in their heyday, automatic washing machines not having yet been invented. Washday was usually on a Monday and was the day to keep out of

Early Musical Beginnings

the house if at all possible. Synthetic fibres had yet to be used to any great extent so most things were made from cotton. Crimplene was still to come, nylon unwearable. Britain was John Bull country and the Empire still very prominent in people's minds. Indian cotton still arrived at Lancashire mills by the Mersey and Manchester Ship Canal every day. Tens of thousands of people worked in mills making everything from shirts to underpants, dresses to ladies knickers or bloomers as we called them. East Midlands towns such as Leicester still had a thriving hosiery industry making socks and stockings whilst closer to home, Walsall still made most leather products sold in the UK. Hong Kong was finding a UK market with its toys and cheap goods but British was still best. Anything else was viewed as inferior and indeed was.

Many people, especially children, were kitted out in home made garments or hand me downs from elder siblings. Rugs were still hand made from rags. I still remember diving into Willenhall baths wearing my home knitted trunks. They disappeared somewhere and floated down to the bottom. All kids were the same. We all had nothing or certainly very little. I don't recall

Early Musical Beginnings

ever being envious of anyone, not at least until the advent of telly – that was still to come, as yet we didn't have one. There was only what we now call BBC 1 and it was only broadcast a few hours a day. Ironically, the next envy I remember was when a friend had a new telly to receive the newly broadcasting ITV. He could watch TARZAN. I couldn't. The downside was that though his dad earned a lot of money, he had to live in India where he managed a rubber plantation.

My dad lived at home. That mattered a lot. Anyway, throughout the 1950's no matter how much money you had, there wasn't a lot to buy apart from everyday requisites. Society was still very much driven by the class system and we were working class. Education was to change all that but we hadn't yet emerged from the system and we were the first generation. Our parents wanted better for us than they had had and they were prepared to work for it.

As I said, the high tech retailer was the laundryman. Usually in ex armed forces vehicles brightly painted they would work door to door down many a street. Sheets of course were not easycare so many households would send them out to the

Early Musical Beginnings

laundry. Our local laundry was the Wolverhampton Steam Laundry Plc. The use of the word "steam" was still seen as having a marketing kudos (though of course marketing hadn't been thought of as a concept). Steam meant, hot, very hot. Steam meant clean. Steam meant hygienic. These were the days when everything was boiled. Washing was done at home and would fill the house with steam. It would run off everything. The more steam the better. Detergents hadn't yet been invented so clothes were still washed with soap. Usually carbolic or Fairy (pictured by a striding baby in a nappy), the soap would be in big bars which my mom or nan would rub on the collars of shirts and the personal parts of underwear. Then they would scrub with a stiff brush until all offending marks were removed. Scrubbing was also done on an old wooden washboard (later to find fame with the "skifflers"). Their hands would be red raw but things had to be clean. When I went to church on Sunday, my shirt had to be the cleanest and most well ironed. My shirt told the world how good a mother my mum was. Prior to rinsing, the washing would be pounded under water by a dolly. The dolly was made of wood, bleached white by use (no bleach in those days). About one and a half

Early Musical Beginnings

metres long or four and a bit feet as we used to measure or a yard and a half (if showing off) the dolly kept mom's arms out of the boling water. As the boiler was gas heated (town gas kept in big vessels called gasometers near the railway) , the streams of hot water rising from the gas fired bottom, would lift the washing to the surface from where mom would plunge it to the bottom again with her dolly. Once satisfied that anything living (lice, nits) must now be dead, mom would use a big pair of wooden pincers to extract the laundry from the boiler and offer it to the mangle. The mangle was a pair of rollers, usually wood, through which she would manually roll the washing, by turning a big iron handle on the side. Most water would be extracted and from there she would peg out on the washing line. My nan had a big mangle about six feet long with rollers held in place by big iron springs. She was well less than five feet tall but would put the washing through on her own. Any man today would complain about such a job, so physical was it, but these were the days pre automation. Electricty was for lighting, precious little else (Bilston still had at least one gas lamp attended twice daily by the gaslighter). I still sing Gene Autry's song

Early Musical Beginnings

"The Old Lamplighter" when I remind my elderly audiences of gas lamps.

The mangle rollers would wear because most use was in the middle of the length and eventually they would need replacing. Also the wood would soak up the liquid over the years and eventually no longer be hard enough to mangle (yes "to mangle" was a verb rather in the same way as to "hoover" would later be). Having been replaced, the old mangle rollers would be cut up and go on the fire (together with pegs, washboard frame and pincers), thereby providing heat for warmth and cooking. The ultimate in recycling.

The laundryman therefore was a godsend. For a few shillings or pence a week, he would take away much of this chore. Folk tended to send the big things, sheets for example, or items that were hard to dry such as towels. Because of pride, my mom would never send anything that looked dirty. If it looked dirty, she would wash it before she sent it! She couldn't risk being seen to be dirty. The laundry would come back parcel wrapped in blue striped paper and tied with white string. Surprising to think that less that fifty years ago, we are predating polythene bags, certainly in

Early Musical Beginnings

common use at least. "Cellophane" had been imvented in 1908 but was still not in everyday use. Mom had to fill in a book saying what she was sending. The same book would be returned with her clean washing. Every item sent would have a little label put on it by the laundry. It was called a Polymark and was personal to each customer, in effect a customer reference code. Thus, when all the sheets were washed together, after ironing, the laundresses (female launderers) would sort them into days, routes and customers by these little numbers. Sometimes the labels came off. Then there was an identity parade, usually on the customers doorstep. My mother of course would refuse any offering until she was satisfied that she had gained a replacement at least as good if not better than the item lost.

Bilston was self contained town. Later to be subsumed into Wolverhampton, (something of great personal distaste to me) it was a Black Country town, part of the Midlands powerhouse driving heavy engineering in Britain. The Black County made anything that could be made in iron or steel. The rag 'n bone man's metal collection went to the blast furnace (Big Bertha) where it was smelted, remade into

Early Musical Beginnings

blocks to be reused. Black Country folk made everything from railway lines to ships anchors and chains, from motorcycles and cars to push bikes and trolley bus parts. Bilston has a manufacturing activity recorded for over 1000 years. Iron and steel works grew out of the ease of access to coal and limestone. Rather than deep mining, Bilston's coal was near the surface so could be mined open cast. Nearby Dudley had heavy limestone deposits. Both were essential in steelmaking. Although on the edge of the Black Country, Bilston boasted much raw material production. Cradley Heath made chains but Bilston made the iron and steel to make them from.

Mines had long gone by the time I was born in 1949, but opposite my house, Stewart and Lloyds had grown into the largest employer in the area. It's existence spawned many workshops, or "shops" as my dad called them where small numbers of people remanufacted the steel into finished goods. Many employees were women who during the war had learned how to operate presses and other machinery traditionally thought of as mans work. Lying between the railway and the cut (canal), Stewart and Lloyds was perfectly located to get product in and out.

Early Musical Beginnings

In the end and many years later, sadly, Bilston folk were to be left facing huge unemployment as it's largest employer, then part of British Steel, finally gave way to foreign competition from eastern Europe and latterly China.

At night, the walls of my bedroom would dance with reflections from the steelworks. The sky was alight and to a stranger must have looked like hell. To me, this was how things were and I thought little of it. Most people love to stare into an open fire. It makes them daydream. For me, Stewart & Lloyds sent me to sleep every night, carried into sleep by my motion picture walls. From 5am each day, my bedroom (pre double glazing days) would echo with the click click of steelworkers clogs. Though I didn't realise at the time, this was music, urban music. A relentless rhythm. When the rhythm died as the shift clocked in, it would be replaced by the metal hammers and rolling machines again all working to clockwork precision. Just like a big bass drum, they would pound through the day, all day. An old air raid siren would announce that the shift had started or ended.

Early Musical Beginnings

In the midst of this industrial inferno, were allotments, a pig farmer, smallholders and green wastelands (now called brownfield sites). In minutes, I could be in green grass with no sign of industry at all. This could be the railway embankment of Bilston or Priestfield or an old industrial site. Locally we had Freezeland and Mars, both aptly named due to waste deposits on their surface. Mars certainly, looked like what I would still imagine Mars to look like. Large boulders, trace streams of solidified metal, engineering debris. A sterile environment? Not to me, it was delight!

Freezland had at it's centre a small pool where we kids would catch sticklebacks and race purple and black coloured cockle shells across the surface. Something lived in these shells once and I guess today they would form part of the "slow food" movement. Here they were, in the middle of all this industrial wasteland which nature had reclaimed. They were rather like oyster shells and we would play D Day landings, lobbing stones at them to sink the landing craft! Newts lived in their hundreds finding homes in old submerged industrial hardware and cast off perambulators. It is ironic that today such an area would be protected a conservation

Early Musical Beginnings

area, an area of "special scientific interest". In the 1950's there they were in the middle of all this industry, all this pollution. Was yesterdays pollution better quality than todays?

Being a one man band as I am now, means collecting interesting pieces of junk that can be used in a musical way – frying pans, tins, saucepans, bits of pipe. Back in the Bilston days, one of my favourite pastimes was "picking the tip". No such thing as recycling centres then. People were positively encouraged to visit the tip and "recycle" things they could use. Many a Saturday afternoon would be spent gathering old valves from televisions or lengths of wood and pram wheels to build that latest "four wheels and a board". I remember once only finding three and I somehow got my dad to help build a "Reliant Robin" version ie one wheel at the front. It was a disaster but that didn't matter. We then tried a "Berkeley" version ie one wheel at the back but that failed too. (Berkeley was a three wheeled sports car).

Together with the brownfield sites, the railway embankment provided what would now be called respite, from the surrounding industrial maelstrom. Here

Early Musical Beginnings

again, rhythm permeated my soul as steam engines rushed through. Clickety click went the express, , clicker..ty....cli....ck went the shunter. Train spotting was a normal, healthy, outdoor and everyday pursuit for most if not all boys. Bilston had a main line to Birmingham and on to London and my books would quickly fill with "spots". No one ever thought to cheat. You had to see it to record it. Cheating was an impossible concept to us; never a thought, it just wasn't done.

At night, the embankment was later to provide refuge as I developed my courting skills. The embankment was private, for kissing and cuddling. If going further was ever intended, a trip to the barbers was needed. He sold the supposedly important "packets of three". French letters we called them. I would wait in the barbers for my haircut. Men before me would be asked "Anything for the weekend, sir". I was never asked and never dared bring the subject up, it was too public. I have no idea if chemists sold the "packets of three". Though I went to the barbers with many an intention, I remained a virgin.

In "rural" terms, the final jewel in Bilston's crown was Hickman Park just down the

Early Musical Beginnings

road from Regent Street where Tommy Burton (the great jazz singer and pianist) lived. Hickman Park had opened 38 years before my birth and now in the 1950's was in it's prime. It was a place for losing oneself in its acres of grassy flatland and tended gardens. It had tennis courts, a fountain and lots of trees. It also had large iron gates which I remember I once had to scale after closing because I had left my jacket in place as a "goalpost" and needed it for school the next day.

Tommy Burton was a teenager when I was born and I knew little of him until later in life when he became one of my musical heroes. I remember seeing him several times with his famous combo in a pub in Wolverhampton playing his stride piano and looking rather like Max Wall with curtain hair. Tommy was a Fats Waller style performer and later in life performed in New Orleans. I heard he was inducted into the New Orleans Hall Of Jazz Fame though I am not sure that is true. Liverpool had the Beatles. Bilston had Tommy Burton. Sadly, I don't think Bilston ever realised the true star value of its Black Country son. Tommy died in September 2000 during a fuel crisis. I celebrate his life every September to this day by singing a

Early Musical Beginnings

Fat Waller song "You Meet The Nicest People In Your Dreams". That was one song I always remember him singing.

Back in the 1950's, every Bilston day was filled with the busyness of life, except Sunday. Sunday was a traditional day of rest. If visitors came they were shown into the front room. This room was used for no other purpose than show. It had the best the family could afford but it was not to be used. I only dared open the door once because with a shared bedroom and my parents chattering in the kitchen, I sought some peace and quiet for schoolwork. I never dared again. My head stung with a swipe. As my mother said "Spare the rod, spoil the child". I was never spoiled.

Sunday was for relaxing and leisure. Men would garden, women would knit. Children would be sent to Sunday School in the afternoon but on return little gardening or knitting seemed to have been done! Sunday for me was three doses of religion and then the weekly disinfection in the tin bath that hung in the back passage. The kitchen would drip with condensation as jug after jug went in the bath and in we kids went, one after the other (or together). Quite early in my life, we had a plumbed in

Early Musical Beginnings

bath upstairs. Just a sink and a bath, no lavatory. That came later.

Unlike today, no inter meal snacking was allowed. Sunday lunch was always THE meal of the week and we were expected to be "clammed" (or clemmed) ie starving. Every last bit had to be eaten and and leftovers denied one the pleasure of pudding.

My parents were not religious. I think the war had knocked it out of them and many others too. They did however take pleasure in my godly pursuits. Everything involved religion. School made me pray, Scouts made me pray, Boys Brigade made me pray. All prayers revolved around being grateful for what we had. At that time, we had very little apart from shelter, food and drink, but questioning the religious line was never a consideration.

Church was fascinating. Not only did it introduce me to singing in public, it educated me in the form of music and it's delivery. I learned to sing with others, to harmonise and to keep time. I learned to read music in a rudimentary way. I knew then that music was my passion though I was to have years of side tracking. At age 9,

Early Musical Beginnings

the choirmaster said that I was good enough to go to cathedral choir school. I was put through the application process and eventually offered a place at Lichfield. But we were working class. Working class boys did not go to boarding school, even if the church was paying.

It was now 1958/9 and I was about to take my 11 plus. The world was changing. Teddy Boys were giving way to beatniks. I think my elder brother Keith was a beatnik. Beatniks I guess were predecessors of hippies, or hipsters as they were called in America. We didn't know that then. Goatee beards and berets combined with intellectual discussion, early beat music, European jazz and academic ambition.

Via Radio Luxembourg, young people were listening to black American music. British youngsters probably heard more black American music than American youngsters did. Aging black singer songwriters like Huddie Ledbetter Leadbelly), found their music in demand in Britain. In these post war years, a cheap ukulele or home made guitar, tea chest bass (Indian tea of course) and moms old washboard made home produced music accessible to the masses. Skiffle was born.

Early Musical Beginnings

All the elments of beatnik were fused into this dynamic syncopated fast and furious rhythm – folk, blues and jazz. Lonnie Donegan was at his peak in the late 1950's with "Rock Island Line", "Cumberland Gap" and more. It is said that Lonnie gave the music the name of skiffle having heard Leadbelly being interviewed on Radio Luxembourg. Leadbelly was asked how he earned a living (remember that black music was still for black people, not white). He apparently replied "Just skuffling man, just skuffling". Apparently, skuffling is slang for busking though one of the free on line dictionaries describes it as *"an energetic attempt to achieve something"*. (I think that definition really captures the essence of skiffle). Across a crackly 208 Medium wave, Lonnie thought Leadbelly said "skiffling". In America, the source music was coming from not only from solo performers such as Leadbelly but from the Jug Band groups such as the Memphis Jugband and Gus Cannon's Jug Stompers; from the early country music of Hank Williams and Jimmie Rogers; from the early folk of Woody Guthrie who was already influencing someone as yet unheard of – Bob Dylan. Fascinating to think that whilst I was in Bilston listening to British skiffle,

Early Musical Beginnings

Dylan was in the USA earning his living in the folk coffee bars singing Woody Guthrie, Jack Elliot and Hank Williams songs and visting the great WG himself in Greystone Psychiatric and Brooklyn State Hospital.

I remember skiffle well. My brother was a huge fan of skiffle as much of it was performed by stripped down jazz bands led by George Melly, Chris Barber and Ken Colyer to name but three. Skiffle erupted with bands such as The Vipers, Les Hobeaux and The Bluegrass Boys. Solo personalities emerged such as Lonnie Donegan, Chas McDevitt, Nancy Whiskey. Many years later, I was to join Chas McDevitt on stage in Shrewsbury and back him with a pretty unimpressive washboard . Oh if I could have the chance again!

Skiffle and Jug Band has remained with me all my life. I still love raw acoustic music particularly when it includes houehold junk – spoons, washboard, gas pipes, jugs, chair legs etc. My personal favourite is the teapot. I play it a lot. I love the sound of authenticity, music from the heart, music as it sounds not as it can be made to sound.

My 11 plus came and went. I passed, so mom & dad said I had to go to Bilston

Early Musical Beginnings

Grammar School and not to Lichfield Cathedral Choir School. I remember the vicar making representations to my parents but it was a useless exercise. My elder brother had gone to Bilston Grammar so if it was good enough for him, it was good enough for me. I didn't argue and tucked away the hurt but it has been like a recurrent sore all my life. Everytime it heals I pick the scab and it starts all over again. How different things would be today. A parent would seize the chance for their child to have such opportunity. This was the 1950's. Going to grammar school was a life changer, an opportunity neither of my parents had enjoyed. They made the decision they thought was right at that time. I paid the price for that decision and it remained one rift with my parents that was never bridged. At the time I was 11 and lived in a society where children did what they were told. Children did not have opinions and parents knew best. Children were seen and not heard.

Music was very important to me as a young man. Whilst my first kiss was to a Beatles song, my musical treasure chest began with skiffle then Elvis Presley and of course Bill Haley and his Comets. My mom and dad and my brother liked Bill Haley. Clearly it

Early Musical Beginnings

wasn't unfashionable then for parents and children to like the same music. We were the upwardly mobile working class. We had a radiogram. No iPods in those days, no cassettes, no mini disc, no CD's. The radiogramme was a cumbersome piece of highly polished furniture. I remember my mom once coming home to find my elder brothers best friend skiffling (dancing) on top of its polished lid. His winklepickers (pointed shoes) and drainpipe trousers convinced my mom that he was on something illegal. It was probably ginger beer but she threw him out anyway. The radiogramme blasted "Rock Around The Clock" from its large mono speaker.

Gene Vincent and Eddie Cochrane were to pass me by. I discovered them much later in life, long after they were gone. My earliest influence must have been Tommy Steele. I remember him "Singing The Blues" and I remember "Little White Bull" as a song and a film. Danny Kaye with his "Ugly Duckling" must have been pouring out of BBC Light Programme because I remember that too!

Ettingshall Primary School in Bilston had engaged me. Conjoined with church, it immersed me in music. It introduced me to

Early Musical Beginnings

English traditional music and dance. Morris dancing was quite common as was sword dancing (not real swords of course, just wooden ones). I remember that we used to dance with our "swords" and end up with them interlaced into a threepenny bit shape. For the unititiated, a threepenny bit was a part of a British currency pre 1971 decimalisation. Also called "thruppence", it was not unlike today's 20 pence coin but thicker and bronze coloured. You could buy a lot with thruppence, a bag of sweets (we called them "suck") was only a penny. There were twelve pennies in a shilling and a shilling would roughly equal 5p today (2007).

Dancing was an everyday part of school life. My song and dance teacher was probably in her late 50's. Her name was Mrs Richardson and she captivated me with her piano and her voice. She would hire a petrol powered

Early Musical Beginnings

chrabanc (coach) and we would go away on interschool dance competitions. We always seemed to win and she always expected us to. We were taught to be competitive and industrious. She expected results and we always seemed to deliver. We used to morris dance with leg bells and coloured scarves. In May, we would ring around the maypole and weave our lattice of ribbon which always seemed to unweave at just the right time. No child could have had better tutor.

At church my choirmaster was an English gent by the name of Frederick Roderick. He always wore a tweed suit and dicky bow tie was very authoritarian. Most adults were in those days. He guided me through Handel's Messiah and the intricacies of timing needed to sing Psalms. He had helped me with my choirschool application even arranging elecution lessons so I didn't speak in Bilston slang. I regretted this in later life because I lost my accent and have to try hard now if I write a song in black country dialect. Under his stewardship, St Leonard's bred fine choristers and I was made to feel the best of the best. I guess I still sing like a chorister which isn't always appropriate to country music or pop! When Mr Roderick retired he was replaced by Mr

Early Musical Beginnings

Bate. I fell for his daughter but that was later. Mr Bate was equally competent and enthusiastic but somehow didn't fire my belly like his predecessor did. Probably it was just me growing up. Teenage years were loomimg and Mr Bate had missed my best. His daughter was lovely though. Sadly she went away to Agricultural College at quite an early age, 16 I think.

So, having passed the dreaded 11 plus, off I went to Bilston Grammar School. It would now be 1960. Skiffle had pretty much gone, though Lonnie lived on. The Beatles hadn't arrived yet. They had been skiffling in Liverpool as The Quarrymen and were then to serve their time in Hamburg. In 1960 they appeared at The Cavern in Liverpool. They were to play there over three hundred times.

Top Ten hits included Elvis with "Are You Lonesome Tonight" and "It's Now Or Never", "Apache" by the Shadows, "Cathy's Clown" The Everly Brothers, "Cryin"and "Only The Lonely" by Roy Orbison. Novelty songs included Lonnie with "My Old Man's A Dustman" and "Itsy Bitsy Teeny Weenie Yellow Polka Dot Bikini" by Brian Hyland . Dance fashions were changing thanks to "The Twist" by

Early Musical Beginnings

Chubby Checker. Mood music continued in the form of "Theme From A Summers Place" by Percy Faith. The old guard hung in with Edith Piaf " Non, Je Regrette Rien". May of 1960 saw George Formby record his last ever single "Banjo Boy" with "Happy Go Lucky Me" on the B side. George's day was done and it is said that this record was cut in one take. He never even took his overcoat off.

Bilston Grammar School served me well as a person but failed me wholesale musically. Grammer Schools in those days were sausage machines for entrance to universtity. Any other goal was seriously less important. They were designed to make you fit the system. Either the classics or science were the chosen subjects. Music, religion, languages and the arts were very secondary or so it seemed to me. I had a friend Stephen, who was an excellent violinist. He seemed to draw strength from the grammar school environment and grow. He went on to study music at University and become a concert performer. I was an "average Joe"; I cannot remember performing, singing or in any way developing from 1960 to 1967/8 when I left the upper sixth.

Early Musical Beginnings

One aspect of my artistic makeup which did grow was during my English literature A level studies. I managed to minimise Shakespeare & Marlowe but pursued D H Lawrence and John Steinbeck. I studied life in urban provincial Britain and the life and times of Woody Guthrie's America. I studied the poems of Lawrence and modern poetry written of the day. In French literature I minimised Moliere and instead read modern day French fiction, Guy de Maupassant and French sex novels.

It was during this time that I made a brief school visit to France. It was my first journey by air and holidaying by such means was in its early life for working class people. I remember we took a charabanc to the south east and boarded a British United DC3 or DC4 in what I recall was little more than a field. It was an old ex RAF ex war aeroplane and seemed to have patches all over its silver fusilage. Seats I recall were little more than slightly uphostered benches not unlike those used in trolley buses. It was cold and noisy. DC 3's were propellor driven aircraft and were used throughout the war by many countries for moving goods and personnel. The end of the war saw many of them sold off into the growing

Early Musical Beginnings

civilian airline business and they found homes all over the world.

It may now be a figment of my imagination but I am sure we "catapulted" off the cliffs of Dover and landed somewhere in a field near Calais where another charabanc picked us up to take us onwards to Paris. This was only 15 or so years on from the end of World War 2 yet I don't recall much evidence of the ravages of war in France's capital city. I do remember the girls whistling at us young lads in the streets of Paris and I do recall that most us us lads smoked. It was considered cool to do so. We smoked our way through Gauloises best and thought we were truly international. Like British Woodbines and Park Drive, Gaulloises were unfiltered cigarettes. Unlike their British alternatives thay were not tightly rolled and they had a very distinctive smell that proclaimed they were foreign. I recall they were packaged in an unusual blue paper pack which for some reason reminded me of the French Foreign Legion. Like most boys, joining the Foreign Legion was a romantic dream to me. Thankfully, smoking Gauloises was the nearest I would ever come to being a Legionnaire!

Early Musical Beginnings

During this time pop music arrived. Everything that made music what it is today was born during that period. English music was pioneered by The Beatles and The Rolling Stones. I became a listener and ceased to be a performer.

My musical tastes were always on the edge of what was going on. I liked some Beatles music. I liked some Rolling Stones. I remember that it was fashionable to like one or the other but rarely both. By the time I was 18, I was a fan of English R&B and early rock. I loved the poetry of folk music and was still ignorant to country music but not as ignorant as I may have thought.

It was the Wulfrun Hall, Wolverhampton, 1964 I think when I first saw the Downliners Sect. They would have been performing together as a band just one year having formed in 1963. Visually, their trademark was the deerstalker hat (Sherlock Holmes hat). My love of the English deerstalker was born. I

Early Musical Beginnings

went to Dunns Gents Outfitter and bought my first deerstalker hat. I still have one today and wore it for a Channel 4 TV programme in 2006/7. The Sect represented everything I liked in music – a driving rhythm, gutsy vocals and they were out on the edge. Alongside the Pretty Things & The Yardbirds, they represented a less commercial alternative to the early Rolling Stones. Never mainstream but all the better for it. To this day, I tend to favour the bands who make up the field rather than those who lead it. They are still hungry, daring, uncomplacent, uncompromising, authentic and true to themselves. Hopefully I still carry that in my music.

Some years later in 1968 I was to see my first One Man Band. Don Partridge had an unexpected number one with his self penned "Rosie" released on Columbia. Partridge, a London busker, with guitar and drum took the pop charts by storm. He was to have a couple of hits then fade to obscurity. I never credit Don Partridge with my love of One Man Band but he must have registered somewhere in my sub conscious. I don't recall any other One Man Bands. My tastes were being fashioned with folk and rock. I was never a follower of any particular band except The Sect.

Early Musical Beginnings

Later I was to be seduced by the sounds of Roy Harper and Michael Chapman, both courtesy of Mazlyn Jones. For now, in the mid sixties it was The Who, The Animals and by 1967, Jimi Hendrix.

Teddy Boys had long gone. Beatniks were a product of my elder brother's generation. Now, in the mid '60's it was the time of Mods and Rockers. In simple terms, mods rode scooters, decorated with as many mirrors as possible. Always dressed smart, a mods trademark "parka" would cover a suit, shirt and tie. Rockers rode motorcycles. They wore leather jackets and were generally seen as unkempt and scruffy.

Many, like me, were mods in appearance only. I never had a fight and generally kept out of trouble. Not that I was a goody goody, I just found it unnatural to reject everything I had grown up with. I came from a decent hard working family, I feared bringing trouble home, not physical fear, just fear of how it might impact on my parents.

I liked having a scooter. I loved embellishing it with spotlights and mirrors.

Early Musical Beginnings

I enjoyed being smart and worked at Craddocks Shoe shop in Wolverhampton in order to save for a top notch parka. I loved the music of the mods. Early R&B, Downliners, Yardbirds, The Who, Small Faces. I had no desire to go to Hastings and fight rockers just because they dressed differently. Rockers tended to cling onto the rock n'roll of the 1950's. That is probably why I don't remember Gene Vincent and Eddie Cochran.

There were no crash helmet laws then. Crash hats as they were called were optional. Older men who rode motorcycles generally wore caps. My dad had a BSA Bantam 125cc. An old 1940's design, it still had a spring saddle rather than a seat. I remember that most Bantams were green.

Early Musical Beginnings

All were two stroke, three gears and with a top speed in the mid 40 mph.

He really wanted a 200cc Velocette (as then ridden by the police). Noddy bikes they were called after the nodding salute a bobby would give if passing a superior officer. They were made in Birmingham. Bantams were also made in Brum as were Nortons. Velocettes were more expensive as they were made in fewer numbers. Dad would take me to the Velocette garage in Parkfield, Bilston and salivate over the water cooled engines. The police liked the water cooled engine because it was quieter. Noddys were often unheard until it was too late (for the criminal).

My dad wore a cap to ride his Bantam. When I went to school on my Lambretta TV175, I still had to wear a green, Bilston Grammar school cap. When out of school I wore my deerstalker.

I travelled miles on my scooter. I even went down the new M1 to London for an interview. I wanted to be a

Early Musical Beginnings

librarian and would spend most Saturdays, all day, in Bilston or Wolverhampton library. Much of this was to do with my A level studies especially D H Lawrence and John Steinbeck. I still love a library today and can happily spend hours in there. Museums never interested me, but the library was an escape for hour upon hour. In those days libraries just offered books. No music. Sadly, they also provided no lavatory and books affect me in that way. I can't be in a library more than a minute before my bowels start protesting. I would spend much time on the floor, forcing back anything that had an exit strategy. At some time, I would have to leave and find somewhere to shed my problem. Once done, life was wonderful and I could concentrate on more important matters. My library ticket was my prize possession. It was appropriaitly coloured - brown.

By 1968 it was time to leave school. In those days, jobs were plentiful. I had failed to get the right grades for university and chose instead to go to work whilst I made my mind up what to do. I intended to resit one A level and hopefully go to Manchester Polytechnic or one of the lesser universities. I had a reserved place at Aberystwyth to study librarianship. Sadly it was never to

Early Musical Beginnings

be. My elder brother had gone to Durham but that was obviously beyond my academic reach. I was too much of a dreamer, didn't find it easy to commit to any study other than what I enjoyed, too fond of girls and then there was the scooter.

A degree in D H Lawrence, John Steinbeck or The Downliners Sect would have caught my interest but these were the days of science and the classics.

University was never to further my education.

I was riding my Lambretta, the day that I met her
I'd been cruising up & down for most the day
She was standing on the roadside, trying to hitch a car ride
So I pulled up by the kerb to have my say
She said thanks for the offer , but you've no need to bovver
I need to be back home by half past ten
The way ahead is hilly and scooters look so silly
There is no way I'll be home by then

(September 1995)

Gay "Pride and Prejucice" 2

It was now 11am. I had been on the seafront of Brighton, dressed in my top hat and tails, for just one hour and it was the hottest day of the year. Within that hour, I had survived being picked up by a Scandinavian, stared at four bare male buttocks protruding from two pairs of cowboy trousers, been intimidated by two ferocious looking but probably harmless lesbians and done a Roger Bannister (he was the first man to run a four minute mile) along

Gay "Pride and Prejucice" 2

Brighton Prom with a bass drum on my back and various other bits of musical parphernalia.

As I looked around me there were clearly two long lines of "floats". I could see neither beginning nor end of either line. Most displays were mounted on vehicles of some sort, mostly lorries and all of them appeared to boast powerful PA systems. In front of was a "Fame" team, behind us was something with a green theme.

"Planet For Sale" a powerful song by my friend Nigel Mazlyn Jones was looping endlessly through my head. The lyric to the song talks about a bankrupt and despoiled world – "Planet For Sale in need of renovation, who'll give us tuppence for a dead old globe". The original version was a soft drum based acoustic ballad but today the "dance" version with its heavy beat was pounding through my consciousness. Brighton certainly wasn't a part of any dead old globe today, certainly not visually. It was bathed in beautiful sunlight and jam packed with beautiful people all pouring out love to Nigel's "sick and old". Or were they part of the problem?

The "Fame" team were lorry mounted and the float presented a collection of young folk all gyrating , some dancing, a few dancing very well, to the "FAME" theme song – "Remember my name, Fame, I'm Gonna Last Forever, I'm gonna learn how to fly, high" or something similar. It was hard to determine individual gender largely because those males who looked female, were of course trying to do so. I must confess that the float was bedecked with pretty people. I saw what I think were ladies dressing as men (and not quite succeeding). Clearly to some folk, today was the big day in their annual calender. I summised that one young lady, at the rear of the float was actually a man. Something about "her" facial features said "Masculine!". Having said that "she" was very pretty and in dancing terms was as feminine as they come. To "her" credit, she danced enthusiastically throughout the parade from before the start to after the official finish line. "Her" hip gyration had to be seen and "she" would have won any TV dance contest. I found it slightly uncomfortable to be fascinated by "her" overt feminine sexuality because deep down I suspected "she" was male. I found "her" quite captivating not least because "she" was in my direct line of sight for the next two hours! Such discomfort happened several times later that day.

The "FAME" team were very loud. I think the PA pushed sound out front and to the rear and I feared that my little banjolele and even my big bass drum would drown in the flood of wattage being generated. It was clear even at this stage that to try and compete would be pointless. I had a word with my fellow artists

Gay "Pride and Prejucice" 2

and advised them that to we would not be heard against such a deluge of sound. We jointly agreed that I would mark time with the Fame music ie keep my drum in time with whatever they were doing. The Mary Poppins dancers, likewise would adjust their dance to suit the rhythm. Should a quiet period come our way, we intended to present the street crowds with our four songs.

Behind our little group were the green group. I think they were either "Jungle Book" or "Good Morning Vietnam". Certainly they looked like animals though they may have been helicopters. Most of them looked green and were sort of dinosaur looking. It seems a little unkind not to recognize what they represented but to be fair to them, I am no expert on musicals and as they were behind me, I spent most of my time looking forwards not behind. I think they were lorry based too though they did have a number of lizard like creatures slithering (on two legs) along the road. Obviously, this was so designed to engage the street audience from close and low. I do recall that most of them were green and scaly hence the lizard description. Still, they could have been helicopters. At least there is a musical to fit helicopters.

My wife and I went to see "Good Morning Vietnam" once in London. We took our two sons. We came out vowing never again to go to

Gay "Pride and Prejucice" 2

another musical. It had received rave reviews and we thought most of it was rubbish. It's success must mean that we were perhaps culturally stunted. I just don't see any point in making a story into a musical unless the music is strong enough to stand on its own without the story. For me, "The Sound of Music" fits this requirement perfectly. Every song is a winner and can stand independent of the other songs and outside the stage show. Vince Hill's huge hit "Edelweiss" is testament to that.

Opera affects me the same way. I have never seen the point in a singing conversation. I realise that I must be missing the point. To spend a couple of hours in a theatre listening to people singing at each other, in a language I do not understand leaves be cold. I would rather listen to a busker in the street, even a bad one! Luciano Pavarotti of course is an exception. Nessun Dorma, the classic aria from Puccini's opera Turandot, which also served as the theme tune for the 1990 World Cup, would make anyone love opera!

Sandwiched between these two was our little group. We comprised – Mary Poppins, half a dozen male chimney sweeps, a couple of outriders (on foot). They walked near the crowd with their promotional banners held high. Additionally, there were various leaflet donors who of course intended to press their giveaway literature into the palms of disinterested or unsuspecting passers by, in the hope that they would subsequently visit the new store in town. I guess that much of this stuff ended up in the roadsweepers bin the next day but today, it mattered. It was afterall the purpose to the day as far as the corporate sponsor was concerned. There was also a young chap in a bowler hat and dark suit. At first I thought he was a dancer but I subsequently believed he too was employed by the sponsor as I don't recall seeing him dance. He seemed to spend a lot of time on his mobile phone, clearly in a business sense. He seemed a thoroughly nice bloke and unquestionably male and later seemed to express some concern as to my physical well being when I began to show signs of exhaustion. I think that as the day ran it's course, I lost all ability to distinguish between male and female but as far as I could establish, all my group were male except Mary of course who was, as far as I know, a young lady of beauty and talent.

I fiddled with my rig. When I step into my One Man Band kit, I cease to be Paul and become "Woody". As today's music was hardly of my choice, I had found it very hard to commit to learning lyrics or indeed the four tunes. As such, I had elected to carry the lyrics and chords with me for quick and easy reference. This is no easy task when walking along playing banjo or guitar and One Man Band and as there were four rather lengthy songs they

Gay "Pride and Prejucice" 2

took up four pages. I had scaled them down from A4 size and printed them onto a bright (pink) Staples card. In order to quickly reference the source documents, I had experimented with several holding mechanisms. The first attempt was a dry cleaners coat hanger modified to prodrude from my mouth truss (more on the truss later) and held in place by two trusty electrical ties. I had straightened the wire hanger and extended it out from my truss so that it provided a fixing point for the card in front of me. Unfortunately, the card was too close for my aging eyes to focus on the text so it proved of little practical use. Had I extended it longer then it would have been a risk to passers by and could have poked a few eyes out. I only had one wire coat hanger at home so my options were limited and the night before leaving Shropshire to head for Brighton, I revisited the problem in something of a panic as I realised that at this time it was now too late to learn the lyrics. I find learning lyrics very hard unless I really want to learn them. Having committed to learn a lyric, I find that one concert performance is worth ten practices at home. In effect, I learn lyrics, live, in front of my audiences. Also, I find that I have to perform a song live several times and often on several instruments, in order to establish what suits it best and in what key I should deliver it. I always seem to sing in a higher key in front of an audience. If the songs are my own, as I create them, I can visualise their delivery in my head. Such visualisation usually incorporates the instrument I intend to play. As such, I usually write a new song using the instrument I intend to play.

The Brighton Pride songs however, were not my own and I suspected that I would never perform them again. The were so unsuitable for a One Man Band. As such, though I had practiced them at home, I had neither the time nor inclination to try them live in my gigs leading up to the Brighton booking. Ironically, in a gig during the week following Brighton, completely unrelated in any way, I was asked if I knew "Supercalifragilistic". It is probably the only time I have declined to sing a request. I was quite astonished at the request and somewhat concerned that someone would think I knew it!

Anyway, re learning the lyrics; in my panic, the night before departure, I had come up with a the idea of one half of a collapsable music stand protruding forwards from my bass drum. As it was at waist height, it gave me extra focus distance but relied on me looking down. I summised that the four songs would take about 15 minutes to perform. With kazoo breaks and a bit of instrumental work, a few bangs, crashes & whistles, I had reckoned I could "One Man Band" them out to about 5 minutes each. Allowing for a break between songs, that would mean twice through each hour. Working on my principle of one live performance equalling ten practices, I guessed that during the first performance I would need the "prompt cards" but by the third time round not need them at all. The advantage of the extending music stand was that having reached that point, I could discard the memory joggers and telescope the music stand back inside the bass drum.

Entertaining people requires confidence in one's own ability. Beyond that, it requires dependable kit. There is nothing more stressful than being let down by one's equipment; breaking strings, amplifier feedback to name but two. I have sweat many buckets during such experiences especially when on stage with a howling mic. Being a One Man Band, technology is not my greatest strength as much of my playing is acoustic. However, of recent years my amplified gig work has increased significantly and so I have "served my time" and found my way out of most if not all problems that lie in wait to ruin a performer. One Man Banding in the streets requires absolute confidence in one's own ability and total faith in one's equipment (more on this later). This I had and I was not surpised that my kit had survived the seaside sprint. Moreover, my extending "prompter" had proved equally dependable and trustworthy and had proved worth the time and thought I had put into it.

I reflected on the lead up to this day.

I had been booked for this event not exactly knowing much about it. Like most things in life, unless they relate to your personal existence, you tend not to notice them. The Americans call this the reticular activating system (RAS) and the best example I can think of is that when you buy a new car you suddenly notice all the identical cars to yours. They were probably there the day before, but the day before the brain screens them out. What little learning I have in this matter informs me that this is the brain's "coping" system. Without it the human brain would be overwhelmed by all the messages it receives from our senses – sight, sound, touch, taste & smell. As such, anything not relevant or necessary to our life at that moment is ignored.

I love some of the words given to scientific issues! For example, instead of writing – sight, sound, touch, taste & smell, I could have written vision, audatory, somatosensory, gustatory and olfactory (to give them there proper names)! Hardly everyday words! Anyway on this day, August 4th, 2007, my vision and auditory senses were working flat out. I suspect that many others that day exhausted their somatosensory and/or

Gay "Pride and Prejucice" 2

gustatory but that is beyond the boundary of my script or the realms of my imagination.

So anyway, in sensory terms my RAS had not much exposed me to either the subject of same sex relationships, cross dressing, gender bending/changing etc etc. As such, today my senses were heightened. All of it was very amusing and to be fair to this hedonistic bunch, they intended it to be entertaining. How for example do you seriously consider the merits of the "**Gay Caravanning and Camping Club**". Clearly, you have to be gay to join but several questions follow on to which I know not the answer :

1. I understand "gay" to mean male so is there a "Lesbian Caravan & Camping Club" with perhaps some sort of affiliation or are women allowed to join and be as "gay" as the men but with women instead?
2. Is the word "Camping" a tenting description or is it defining entry as requiring a gay person to "camp up" their appearance or demeanour?
3. Are motorhomers and camper van owners included?
4. Remembering my friends misdemeanour, are pets allowed especially Alsation dogs?
5. Are there "gay" sites and if so, what are the criteria for site inclusion? Also,

would there be a "gay" sites handbook? Perhaps a pink one with pretty pictures?
6. How is the membership fee paid??
7. What about cross dressers, transexuals etc? Perhaps there is a "Cross Dressers and Transexual Caravanning & Camping Club?"
8. What about equal rights? A "straight" person may wish to join. I can't for the life of me imagine why, but who knows. Perhaps like John Leslie who fell from TV grace because of a rape accusation or Gary Glitter with his child porn such a person may be researching a book or researching an acting part? What a wonderful pick up line - *"I'm not gay but may I sleep with you tonight for research purposes?"*

Towards the front of the parade were the gay **Police Force** members led by their presumably gay Commander or Chief Constable, not sure which. The concept of a gay policeman seems rather odd to me yet there is no reason I suppose why it should. Same sex relationships obviously exist in every walk of life, the police force included. Yet again though, questions are raised :
1. If someone is arrested and they are required to remove their clothes, be strip searched or in some other way reveal their nakedness, would they wish to do that to a gay "Officer Of the Law"?

Indeed should they be required to or are their Human Rights being compromised? If you personalise the question, ie in my case let's say my wife was the arrested offendor, whilst she would not be expected to strip off in front of a male officer, equally, she would be similarly concerned at stripping off in front of a lesbian officer. Unfortunately, in the latter case, she would have no way of knowing the officer was so inclined, BUT, should she have the right to know?

2. If gay and lesbian officers can be admitted to the force, are cross dressers and transexuals excluded?
3. What goes on in the changing rooms?

Other gay and lesbian public servants seemed to include both paramedics and fire officers. I say seemed to, because of course there is no way of knowing and I'm not sure it matters anyway. I do think that there are certain issues to be considered as already mentioned, but, I suppose where emergency services are concerned, they are a good example to us all that sexuality should not matter, it should be secondary to their professional calling.

Another interesting float was the **"Gay Line Dancing Club"**. They were superb dancers, fantastically turned out and as camp as they come. Any modern day "Carry On Film" would find a home for their contribution. They were so good that I wondered whether they entered competitions and if so, what the "Westerners" made of them. Being an entertainer, I often go to "Western" events. As much as being gay may seem odd to someone that is straight, how do you comprehend a "Westerner".

For the uninitiated, in the UK, a "Westerner" is someone who either dresses up or lives as closely as they can the life of someone out in the late 20th century Wild West of America. They tote guns (replicas) , some live in wigwams as Indians (red ones, not the ones who invented Baltis) and some live in cabins as settlers and homesteaders. Some cabins are on caravan chassis. All are as authentic as something American but made in the UK can be. I guess the "hobby" has grown out of Country and Western music.

I go to Welshpool Country & Western Music Festival every year. A fabulous event. The Indians perform all their traditional dances. On the cowboy front, there are fast draw competitions and much conversation is had about actions, draw speeds, gun types etc. You can see cowhands, sheriffs, Bible carrying Reverand's, Unionists, Confederates, Indians. The festival opens with all of them running down the hill from Powys Castle with flags waving and guns firing. During the festival are merchants selling every type of western article imaginable – music, guns, clothing, memorabilia etc. The festival ends with a lowering of standards in the concert arena. These people take it very seriously, yet Monday to Friday, I guess many are businessmen, bankers, factory workers, office staff, retired folk etc. They are just another example of the quirkiness of the UK population. I have often wondered if an English Robin Hood Society or Reliant Robin Club or something else very English exists in America!

I suppose to be fair, most young boys who in 2007 are now aged 55 plus will have grown up with early BBC and later ITV television. We were the generation that was weaned on to TV as a medium. We were certainly never force fed, we took as much as we could get and much of it was US inspired – initially Gene Autry, Tex Ritter, Roy Rogers and latterly John Wayne in more cowboy films than any one of can remember. Also, as children, the UK cinema was at it's peak. Following the austerity of immediate post war years, the growing disposable incomes in the 1950's afforded trips to the cinema not least of which, for us kids was the Saturday matinee where many of the B movies (yes you got two films in those day plus PATHE News) were "Wild West" films. So it seems, the love of cowboys and indians, cultivated in our 1950's boyhood, manifests itself today in the "Westerners" clubs.

Brighton Pride was full of theatrical types. I recall one gentleman, very scantily clad, of mixed race origin. He gave me a whistle on a white ribbon. He spent his time working the crowds and disposing of his whistles. They seemed to be the special giveaway of the day and as the parade was to wear on, proved to deliver a collective noise of quite deafening proportion. There turned out to be dozens of whistle givers. All were startlingly dressed or undressed as the case may be. The rules of the day forbade nudity but I certainly saw one naked man. It seemed that that was he was known to do best – be naked. I recall that he walked along with a discreetly positioned cap or hat. Whether he ever dropped it I never found out but he certainly delighted the street crowds.

Another bloke, with next to nothing on was wearing a pair of "stilt" like extensions on his feet. They seemed to be of a bendy metal and he literally bounced around the street covering huge distances with each bounce.

Although these characters wore very little, what they did wear was worn to thrill, impress, seduce, fascinate and captivate. Mohican haircuts, purple orange and pink locks, kilts, outrageous dresses, ostrich feathers in profusion. In fact the more flamboyant the better.

Many facets of city social life were on show : the City Of Brighton Gay Mens Chorus were an authentic, quality male voice choir, as good as any : the Lesbian and Gay Christians were unafraid to proclaim both their faith and their sexual leaning ; I recall some sort of Trade Union of Lesbian, Gay, Bisexual and Transgender Members : the Dancing Dorothy's were presumably some sort of dance club and were beautifully attired in their blue gingham frocks.

One thing I began to notice were enormous eye lashes, that is on those gentlemen dressing as ladies. Kenny Everett would have been there were he alive. He would have done Brighton "in the best possible taste". All girly things were done to excess and eyelashes and makeup were no exception. This was the day of the Brighton calender and I felt I had not done it proud in my lack of preparation. Having said that, my attire was unique. No one else was anywhere near my appearance and I was every inch the Englishman.

I became aware of the gay security guards orgainising the departure of the leading floats. I remembered three large "ladies" in a large open top car passing by and guessed they were leading the parade off, probably followed by

Gay "Pride and Prejucice" 2

the gay police officers. I remembered my sponsor telling me I was leading the parade though I had already realised that my job was to lead their contribution to the parade, not to lead the actual parade! I was quite happy about this. The less attention I drew, the happier I thought I would be.

One by one the floats kicked into action. The music blared, the dancers danced. Soon it was our turn and I set out with a firm step and at a pace that worried me - but I had to keep up. The "Fame" float blared it's music out but at this stage we were not yet even at the start line. We soon ground to a halt. As I looked around I realised that there were thousands of people lining the starting point. I had no idea of the route, no idea where my wife was nor our motorhome. I guessed as long as I "followed the leader" I would get to our destination. The cacophony of sound was deafening. Thousands of whistles, screams, cheering, shouting, float music and my drum. As I looked up I could see that Brighton front had a sharp right turn ahead and a road that seemed to run upwards but parallel to the promenade. Above me was a sea of faces and as is the way with the human race, no two were the same. It reminded me of the funeral of Diana, the Princess of Wales, such was the number of people lining the street.

Gay "Pride and Prejucice" 2

Eventually, we reached the point where I had originally been left by Sea World. I chose not to search the crowd for my new Scandinavian friend. The "bummers" were nowhere within my view nor were the intimidating lesbian ladies. This was a strange crowd. As well as the gay community, there were everyday folk – the old, the young, the disabled, children of every age, some on their fathers shoulders, some in pushchairs. Straight stood alongside gay in perfect harmony, no preconceptions, no judgement, no conflict. I realsed that Brighton was displaying what many cities never achieve, absolute harmony of it's citizens. I realise that it may not be like that all the time, but all these straight folk had come to see the sights knowing full well what they were in for. Indeed that was why they had come.

The thought struck me that this gay community welcomed us straight folk with open arms. We were not prejudged as we might prejudge them. They were celebrating their sexuality and were proud to include us in their day.

I became aware of an African gentleman, with very little on - bare chested, body piercings everywhere and a short dress. He was overtly feminine and played the crowd like a finely tuned instrument. The crowd loved him and he was clearly having the time of his life.

Gay "Pride and Prejucice" 2

The Fame tune repeated on and on. I kept the beat for my dancers to follow. I had realised that to play my banjolele loud enough for even me to hear would simply wear the skin from my finger. I guess by now that I was pretty much miming except for the drum. The crowds seemed to love my siren whistle. I had bought it off eBay perhaps two years before Brighton. It was made by the world famous comany, with a comic book name – ACME. ACME I had learned is still a worldwide manufacturer and seller of a diverse range of goods. Apparently it began life providing corks and flypaper to bug collectors. It has some sort of link with Warner Bros and sells everything from birdseed to Batman outfits. Anyway my ACME siren whistle was loud enough even to rise above all these thousands of whistles that absolutely everyone seemed to be blowing. My ACME whistle seemed to earn me a great deal of respect that day. It was unique in a world of whistles!

The fact that I was a One Man Band certainly caught people's attention. It was a pity that they could not hear me but that didn't seem to matter. Occasionally I "worked" each side of the thoroughfare. Though I haven't mentioned it, it is probably obvious that we, the parade, were on the street and it was lined both sides with thousands of people. We were well covered by security who worked hard to stop bystanders swelling the ranks of the parade. A few did slip through. I recall one "lady" joining me to play the spoons to my beat. Unfortunately "she" had forgotton them so just went through the motions. I play the spoons, have done for years. We were equally surprised that in this maelestrom of humanity two spoon players had somehow found each other.

My dad used to play the spoons, the bones, comb/paper and harmonica. I always think it sad that he never lived to see me do the same. Every Christmas, all these bits and pieces would come out and within minutes, even having not played for twelve months, the Christmas carols would have musical accompaniment. Of course, I was a teenager then. This was the era of the Rolling Stones and The Beatles. I had no interest at all in spoons or bones. Years later, I was to learn both and am now an accomplished player of both.

The spoon miming "lady" was joined by her husband, a large, loud and jolly man. Both of them danced and soon merged into the parade. He wore a garland of flowers around his neck and together with his shorts looked quite Hawaian. With weather like this, we could have been in Hawaii. The sweat was pouring down my legs. Thank goodness that underneath my tailcoat I had elected to wear shorts.

Gay "Pride and Prejucice" 2

I became aware that my morris dancers leg bells had become unvelcro'd. I later learned that I had lost two of my large bells. Someone elses gain if they appreciated bells! I edged to the side of the parade and politely asked a neutral looking person to reaffix them. She did the best she could but they came undone again. Worse still, I was now behind the very group I was supposed to be leading so I had to run to catch them up.

The sponsor had now provided a supply of bottled water. I had my own in a screw top metal flask but we never stopped long enough to unscrew the cap. That was my lesson for the day. My flask hangs from my One Man Band. It has served me well over the years but of course I had never before been in a parade. In previous street festivals, I worked alone, stopping and starting at leisure (and singing my own choice of songs). Here, I was but a tiny part of a huge moving creature whose beginning and end were beyond my view. The bottled water on offer was very welcome. I regretted bringing my own. The weight of my rig was now beginning to tell and the flask did not help. It banged into my thigh with each relentless step and there was no time to stop and remove it. Even had there been, I had nowhere else to put it. My One Man Band of course was not designed for hiking. Shuffling yes, hiking no.

Gay "Pride and Prejucice" 2

We were now in what I presumed to be the High Street. Above the City Centre shops were flats and letting rooms. Many of them had balconies and today each one was packed with young people. It occurred to me that nothing had been thrown. No peanuts, no fag ends, no tomatoes. Yet, we were sitting ducks and in this crowd no one would ever have discovered the perpetrator. Brighton's population deserves much credit for that. In most places I would have expected something to be lobbed especially as the alcohol had it's effect as well as any other of the many substances that I guess were available that day. Thanks Brighton, I appreciated not being hit by a tomato!

I asked the chap in the bowler hat (who seemed official), how much further we had to go. He pointed to what I think was a viaduct and said that we were about two thirds of the way and that the viaduct was the end. It seemed a long way away and the relentless plodding was wearing me down. The dancers behind had been worn down to fatigued statues. The crowds had loved them. Their dress, their dancing ability, their willingness to perform had charmed everyone who saw them.

I decided to break the monotony working on the theory that a change was as good as a rest. I worked my way to the right hand edge of the

Gay "Pride and Prejucice" 2

group and broke into Blue Suede Shoes. The lady in front of me loved it and immediately joined in. Unfortunately without amplification, amongst this crowd of thousands (reputedly 150,000), she was the only one who could hear me. Very quickly I risked being left behind again & I noticed that my dancers were once more performing, in spite of my absence. I rushed to join them and decided that to entertain one person properly was pointless when so many more would have no idea at all what I was doing.

The viaduct did look nearer. Not much, but certainly nearer. My face was now boiled, quite literally. I had perspired profusely and such was the sun that it had literally boiled the liquid on my face. I must have looked very red. Just then I saw my wife in the crowd and realised that I must have been towards the end. Later, she was to remark how safe she felt in this crowd of thousands. She had parked up the motorhome in the park and was escorted to the official end point of the parade. From there, she had worked a little way down the street to gain a good view. At four foot ten inches, she has to position herself well if she is ever to see anything. She found herself in eminently gay company, literally, but was made extremely welcome, even as a stranger.

It was a joy to see her. I realised how tired I was and how I had been running on reserve. I was exhausted. Suddenly the viaduct was just in front of me. It reared large into the Brighton skyline. After what seemed like forever, it was now above me and still we were going. I broke into an old skiffle / jug band song "Wild About My Lovin'" again pulling from my very bootstraps. Still we went on. My bowler hatted friend was as confused as me. It should now be over but we were still going. Suddenly we were in the park and I could see my motorhome "Woodys One Man Band" emblazoned on the side. Then we were past it and still going.

Then we stopped. I had long lost Jill my wife. She had been consumed by the crowd. I became aware of people messing with my rear, my drum that is. A group behind me asked me for a song. I replied that I was exhausted. They called me a miserable old bastard and they were probably right at that time! I could see the motorhome but in this crowd, with a drum on my back, there was simply no chance. Furthermore, all the performers behind my little group were still piling into this congested area, floats to the left, pedestrian traffic to the right. I could see the Rocky Horror Show float but was too concerned at my own predicament to be much interested. A policeman close by spotted my isolation and waved two security staff for their help. The three of them encircled me and assisted me through the crowd to the other side of the roadway down which the parade was still coming. Once beyond the perimeter, they were suddenly gone, obviously beckoned by their next job and I was free of the crowd.

I worked my way to the motorhome, saw the door open and pretty much collapsed against the door. For me, Brighton Pride, 2007 was over. Another gig was done. Though I didn't know it, I had lost 6lbs in weight. I shed my drum with relief and dropped into a chair on the grass. I looked at it, still as good as the day I last "re-engineered"it. It had survived, like me, a two hour, two mile trek through tens of thousands of people on the hottest day of the year. Nothing had broken and apart from two morris bells, nothing had dropped off.

I reflected on my day. I had not looked forward to it yet I had thoroughly enjoyed it. I had not looked forward to a "gay" parade yet this was no different to any other festival. Folk were here to have fun and enjoy themselves. Ok their way might be different than mine but so what. I continued to observe the many facets of human sexuality as I sat in the sun, in my chair savouring my day. In front of me a family picnicked. Beyond them, a group of youngsters sat and drank and had fun. Some were straight, some were gay but they were all friends with each other. I thought about prejudice and how so often it emanates from us older folk. Youngsters today grow up in a more open

Gay "Pride and Prejucice" 2

environment. When I was a child my parents told me to steer clear of the public lavatories at the top of Bilston High Street. Men is gaberdine macs hung about outside. The kids called them queers but we didn't really know what they were, just that their favourite building was the lavatory!

Hopefully today, youngsters grow up in a more tolerant and more understanding environment. They are racially aware and sexually aware. Equally, most of them are tolerant of each other. My experience of Brighton Pride continued as the last of the parade walkers filed past. My brain, as always turned to music. I wrote a song. Clearly it was influenced by my day.

Charlene is a man, born Charles Edward Lee
A child of the postwar years, 1953
He had 16 years being a boy and 5 years being a guy
Then he fell in love with Maybeline, they married one July
He loved her silky dresses, they stirred him when he touched
But the day he tried to wear one, Charles Edward Lee went butch.

So he bought some wigs, he bought some hose
Bbought some high heels too
And as Charlie became Charlene
His friends they numbered few.
He was the only man in woman's clothes
To walk the streets that day
And everyone who saw him laughed
Pointed, called him gay
But Charlie still loved Maybeline, he wasn't gay at all
He just liked wearing women's clothes STRANGE, *him being 6ft 4*

Gay "Pride and Prejucice" 2

For Maybeline life was hard being married to Charlene
Her love was strong, she saw no wrong
Even though he was a queen
They heard out east were similar folk all living in one place
Some like them, some different, all living in God's grace.
Withorange hair and bright red lips
Their choices they were few
And at 6 ft 4 with size 10 feet, folk held a point of view.

Now when they go out they turn some heads
Both male and female gender
They share their makeup and their scent
When going on a bender
They do no harm, they're just different
It's hard to tell who's who
'Cept Charlene is so tall, Maybeline 5ft 2.
It might seem odd to you and I why one should make such choice
Especially when Charlene, has Charlies deep bass voice.

Beauty comes in many forms, black, white, straight or gay
And Charlene was born Charles but had to turn away
He didn't choose the way he is, his cards were dealt at birth
But dressing up with Maybeline he found his own self worth
He is what he is, in that he has no say
Whatever we each are, God made us all that way

Charlene is a man, born Charles Edward Lee
But now he's known as Charlene and that's ok by me.
How about you?

Oh yes, I forgot. I never did see Max Millers statue!!

A Young Man's Years

1967 saw my schooldays come to an end. Friends went off to university, to college and into work. I chose the latter, not becuase I didn't want further education, but rather because I didn't know what I wanted to do. Grammar School had spent seven years telling me that I should go to a good university and offering no alternative if I did not. Anyone who did not go to university was deemed a failure. My elder brother had gone to Durham and visiting that beautiful city had become a part of my family's life. My parents had owned a car for some years now (a 3 gear Ford Prefect and then a Singer Gazelle) and so filling and emptying my brothers college rooms at beginning and end of each term were part of the family routine. I really would have liked to go to university but I had not achieved the grades I needed.

My years at grammar school had enriched me in many ways and even now, I recognise that much of what I enjoy in the world of literature and language, results from those years. In other ways, I now reflect back and realise that I had become stunted in so many other ways. Firstly, the school was an all boys establishment so mixing with the opposite sex had never been easy and never been encouraged. Any musical ability that had been cultivated at primary school had long since been scourged from my being. Emotional development was not foremost in all boys

A Young Man's Years

grammar school so arts were secondary to traditional subjects.

I was now a young man, eighteen years old and needing to make decisions. Society dictated education or work. Boys or girls of working class parentage were mostly unaware of the options of a year off, or travel or voluntary work in some foreign clime. It is not to say that such options did not exist, but to a boy from Bilston they were never visible, never a real option, never on my radar and were never at my conscious level as being a real choice.

I decided to go to work, at least until I made my mind up what else to do. I was no stranger to work. Craddocks Shoe shop had provided school time Saturday work from the age of 16. In sixth form school holidays I had worked for a civil engineering company in Brierley Hill near to where my father worked. I was a labourer and worked with a bad mouthed man called Jimmy Plant. He claimed to be Robert Plant's father (of Led Zeppelin fame) but I have no way of knowing whether that was true or not. Although Jimmy had a foul mouth, he had a heart of gold and introduced me to the world of the industrial working man. I spoke very differently to him. His every second word used bad language and I never swore, still don't. He was a Black Country man with a broad accent. My accent had long since been "elecuted" out

A Young Man's Years

of me when preparing for choir school. His favourite word began with "f" and he never exhausted the way in which it could be used. Jimmy was head labourer and responsible to Bill, the foreman. As a foreman, Bill was entitled to wear a brown warehouse coat or "cow gown" as they were called, a shirt and tie and shoes. Jimmy had to wear navy blue cotton boilersuits, big workmen's boots and an old sweater. Bill had an office with a fire. Jimmy had a shed with a coke burner.

Working with Jimmy made me revisit the basics of human life – food , drink, shelter and warmth. He was a hard worker, always hated the bosses and took every opportunity to tell them. So industrious was he, that in spite of his vitriolic tongue, he never lost his job. A bit like Billy Connolly, he could call someone a bastard without causing them any offence, except Bill. Bill was pretty useless and I think he knew it. His only useful role as far as I could see was to fill his khaki cow gown with his portly frame. He seemed to know very little and successfully did nothing. He survived entirely on the ability of those below him. He had ginger hair which set him apart from the rest. His hair colouring always found it's way into any discussion of his uselessness. "F..ing ginger b....stard" Jimmy would say. The working man of the late 1960's and early 1970's had not yet been educated in tolerance or political correctness. Black people were niggers, gays were queer or homo's and Bill was a "ginger b....stard". Also he was

A Young Man's Years

uncannilly like captain Mainwaring of Dads Army fame.

Jimmy taught me the intricacies of a coke burner. How to stoke, how to control the heat with airflow and most importantly how to seemingly make a shovel of fuel last all day. The burner was made of iron and stood pride of place in our shed (yes I was included as one of the menfolk). For some reason Jimmy never turned his vitriole on me. Though he knew me to be different, not least of which because my dad collected me in a car whilst he still walked everywhere, he never singled me out for fun. Contrary to this, he almost seemed to take me under his wing and regard me as some sort of working mans social project. Protege would be too strong a word but he did look out for me and seemed to genuinly like me even though I had been well educated, had long hair and spoke differently.

It was working with Jimmy that made me realise that I was no longer working class. Education had set me apart from my roots. I wouldn't say that I was middle class, but I had been educated at grammar school, had O'levels and A levels, my parents owned their own house, my dad drove a car and went to work in a tie, my brother was at university. I spoke French, I read poetry and I could talk literature.

A Young Man's Years

Jimmy never spoke literature at least not to me. He had heard of D H Lawrence, but for all the wrong reasons. His only goading of me was to do with education. He came from a school of thought that believed education did not make the man. Experience, age common sense and wisdom made the man. For him, literature began and ended at the tabloids. He roughly ripped out all the Page 3 pin ups and stuck them around his shed. Together with "Health and Efficiency" and anything else he could lay his hands on, the shed was a who's who of porn and female nakedness.

Reading the Daily Mirror was usually done at the same time as cooking the bacon and boiling the water for the tea. Both were done on the coke fire. The old brown kettle stood on the top puffing steam continuously. The bacon was put on a small coal shovel and placed in the fire, on the red hot coals. Fat would run off the shovel and into the flames where it spat and hissed like a cornered cat. No bacon ever tasted better that that from Jimmy's shovel. Between two hunks of rough cut bread it would meet the highest culinary expectation. Though I didn't think of it at the time, I never bought any bacon or tea. Jimmy must have provided everything. It was as though I was a guest in his shed. Tea from Jimmy's kettle had no equal, so much so, that unable to match it, I later switched to coffee and to this day very rarely drink tea.

A Young Man's Years

Working for a Civil Engineers, as a yard worker, we handled all the building product returned from site – acrow struts, trench sheets and wood. All were "filed" around the yard in their various locations and our job was to ensure that they were made usable for the next job. There was nothing in the way of sophistication, no material handling aids, no machinery. On a work site, trench sheets were driven into the ground around the inner perimeter of a trench. Their function was to provide a retaining wall to keep the surrounding earth from caving in on those working in the trench. To keep the sheets apart and provide safe working, struts would be extended inside the trench from one side to the other so keeping the trench sheet walls apart. The trench sheets interlocked. The struts adjusted by way of a screw handle. Sheets would be driven into the ground with the bucket of a digger or a weight on the end of a crane. No finesse was employed and sheets would be severely damaged at each end. The metal sheets were about half to three quarters of an inch thick and in varying lengths.

Often the trench void would be filled with concrete and then the sheets withdrawn by crane. Each sheet had a hole in it's end of about two inches in diameter. A chain would be passed through the hole and secured to the crane which would then literally tug the sheet

A Young Man's Years

out of the ground. If done by a digger, the reach was much less so the sheet would be tugged out at an angle rather than directly from above. As such, the sheets would arrive back at the yard, bent, buckled and damaged. They were incapable of interlocking without reparation.

Repairing them was done with a sledgehammer and heat. Jimmy was about four feet ten inches high with a low centre of gravity. He could swing a sledge better than any man and could make good these sheets, (which today would be scrapped), in no time at all. By contrast, I found this a hugely difficult job and nothing at school had prepared me for such labour. Jimmy was always careful to ensure that our repaired sheets went on one pile so that when Bill wandered around he would see two men, but only one pile. Jimmy worked all the harder to ensure that the pile represented two mens work and not one and a half. The pile comprised sheets laid one on top of the other. No gloves were available so there were many trapped fingers and blood blisters, always on my part as Jimmy's hands were like leather.

Acrow struts often found themselves being extracted from a trench, now kept apart by poured concrete. Once out, they would be cast aside and eventually loaded on a lorry to come back to the yard. They could lie on site for

A Young Man's Years

weeks by which time the conrete had set hard. Once hard, the concrete prevented the handle from turning on the screw and therefore the strut would not extend. Armed with six inch nails and a hammer, Jimmy and I would labour all day, outside, whatever the weather, carefully hammering the concrete out of the screw thread. Sometimes the concrete was in such volume that you couldn't even see the screw thread. On such occasions we had a drum of particularly viscious acid. I think it was hydrochloric.. nasty stuff, it would burn right through your clothes or shoes and several men ended up at hospital where they would be dressed and returned to work. No sick pay then, No work, no pay!

Driving a six inch nail along a thread in January or February, in the snow or rain or intense cold was about as miserable a job as I have ever had. My fingers would jar with each blow and my fingers would be numb. After cleaning the thread we had to "paint" the thread with a coating of old oil to make the thread easy to wind. If repairing trench sheets, every landing of the sledge would send tremors through my every bone and though I never wished I was dead, I think I would if I had to do it now! Bill would be warm in his office whilst Jimmy and I would be frozen.

Jimmy must have taught me part of my work ethic. If you are ill, go to work, if you are cold,

A Young Man's Years

work harder, if you are tired break the monotony with more work, just a different task. Never take time off, never succumb and always be prepared to do more than is expected. I am sure that Jimmy is with his maker now. He will still be swearing, but he will be the best worker God ever had. Under Jimmy's protective wing, I could easily have stayed beyond what became an extended final school holiday of almost a year. Eventually, Jimmy was to encourage me to step out in the world and make some decisions.

Another visitor to our shed was Dick. Dick drove a firms lorry. It was an ex war AEC Matador, one of the most famous vehicles of World War Two. Built by the Associated Equipment Company who also made London's famous red bus, the Matador was built to tow artillery along road and across rough terrain. Above the passenger seat was a screw lid in the roof where the machine gunner would have stood surveying hostile territory. Post war, the Armed Forces shrunk its peacetime vehicle and armoury inventory and many Matadors found their way, via Government auction, into private industry, Cheap to buy, they were easy to maintain by the many ex sericemen now in

A Young Man's Years

civvy street and they were versatile in use. Dick drove such a truck. These vehicles predated synchronised gears and he would literally stand on the clutch to change gear. I recall it had a top speed of some 30mph and towed a trailer.

Dick was a gypsy. He smoked roll ups as everyone else did, me included. His roll ups were different though. They, like him, looked dirty and dishevilled. Dick had a shifty look about him as though he was dodging a pursuer. Always on the lookout. He also wore an earing, something I had never seen on a man before. He wore a long mac, whatever the weather, a bit Clint Eastwood style. In fact he was very like Clint. His eyes were creased with squinting. His face was gnarled and ruddy, suggesting many fights. His hands, probably unlike Clint, were black with work, with broken finger nails and tough leathery skin. Dick carried a knife, not unusual in those days, but in his case I always guessed it might be put to purposes other than slicing a tomato. He was thin and wiry and was self conscious in my presence.

Eventually, I was told to stand in as a drivers mate. As drivers mate my job was to stop traffic so we could go around a traffic island the wrong way or ask vehicles to move out of the way. This was a long heavy haulage rig and was not designed to fit urban roads which

A Young Man's Years

in those days were not built to cope with heavy traffic. Sometimes we had a police escort. Then, I would just sit and observe. The driver was Dick. He was a dirty bugger. I never saw him wash. Even when we stayed away at night in cheap hostelries and transport B&B's, I never saw him take even his mac off. He was high.

On the positive side, like Jimmy, Dick had a tremendous work ethic. If we were away from home we would work at least ten hours a day. Even though it couldn't be proved (these were pre tacho days), for Dick it was all about self worth and although I suspected he was not averse to the odd criminal activity, he was as honest in his work as the day was long. He would always be up at six. He even slept with his shoes on though he did unlace them. He lay between the sheets but fully dressed as though he might be called upon to be in action in seconds. I suspected this was related to his war activities or National Service training. He never talked about either, but perhaps he was used to sleeping fully dressed and being ready to go into action instantly upon waking. By two minutes past, he was going for breakfast. I never saw him clean his teeth. He used to chew twist and his teeth were brown. (Twist was a chewable form of tobacco leaf, a bit like a rope of tobacco). We would usually work until 7pm. Hard physical work, manhandling heavy chain, one link of which would test most men. Dick just took it in his stride. "Yow con kid

A Young Man's Years

other people but yow conna kid yowerself". He was a Black Country man. He worked hard all day and drank around thirteen pints every night.

The relationship between Jimmy, Dick and to some extent my young self was based on respect. Respect was earned not bought, not given. I remember once at the yard jumping onto a six inch nail. It went through the sole of my boot and up, through and out the top of my foot. I shouted for Jimmy who pulled me off the nail. The blood spurted and my foot was wrapped in a rag. I went to hospital for a tetanus injection and two big plasters. An hour later I was back at work. That earned respect. I actually think Jimmy was proud of me, thought he had taught me well. Dick became much less guarded in my company after that just as though I had proved myself. I remember that I limped for a while but I told my mom I had banged my leg. She never knew about the nail and I never chose to tell her. It was mans stuff. My dad knew but I think he kept it a secret too.

One job I was sent on was to labour at a site in Codsall. They were extending a sewage farm to serve the growing population. I remember that Dick used to wade through the excrement and pluck big juicy tomatoes from the plants that were growing. I don't know about today, but in those days, tomatoes were immune to

A Young Man's Years

sewage treatment and the finest specimens grew out of the circles of human waste. Dick would stand in these circular pools of excrement and polish off one tomato after another. If he had a sandwich, he would wade back "to shore", extract his trusty knife and slice the tomato onto thick slices of bread or "doorsteps".

I recall some years later fitting a towel roll machine in the workshop of a knackers yard. As I was there I became morbidly fascinated by the dismemberment of a cow. It arrived in the back of lorry bloated and stiff. It was hauled out by its stiff back legs which were chained to a winch. Lying on the workshop floor, it was then "butchered" by the yard staff. Their first job was to slit its belly and haul out the innards. There were metres of them, like a long chain. The smell was grotesque yet somehow I was transfixed. The carcase was quickly seperated but to what end I am not sure. In those days, the best cuts still found their way (illegally) into the food chain, sold to unscrupulous market traders who knocked them out at cheap prices. People hadn't forgotten the war years. Meat had been scarce. Other parts went to the pet food industry, some into livestock supplements. Other pieces went to the maggot yards to be blown by bluebottles to produce fishing flies. Hides of course went to the tannery, another foul smelling place. I recall that the hooter sounded

A Young Man's Years

for lunch break and one yardman remained in the workshop amongst the blood and guts. He calmly got his sandwiches from an old army haversack which he used as a snap bag. The knife that he had slit the cow with was wiped on his moleskin trousers and then he used it to peel an apple. I think I was in shock. Somehow amongst all this carnage, all this blood, all this offal, all this death and mortuary practice, the idea of eating an apple with its skin on was unacceptable!

Resulting from Jimmy's constant badgering, I decided during my time at Codsall what course of career I would like to follow and that was tourism. I had not secured the grades to go to University to study librarianship, I had grown through the period of wanting to be a monk, Trinity House had offered little career opportunity as an inland lighthouse keeper and I had no skills to earn a living as a Welsh hill farmer. Following an altercation with my parents, university in any form was not a financial option, so being independent, I decided to make my own way. The 1970's predated courses in tourism and the Midlands technical colleges were still focussed on Midlands trades, especially engineering. The Midlands was still the powerhouse of the UK, though cracks were obviously beginning to appear. I got a place to study tourism at Manchester but without parental help, it was not option. Perhaps looking back it was , but

A Young Man's Years

to me it seemed out of reach. It could be argued that I gave up too easily. I would accept that criticism because I honestly cannot remember whether I did or not. I decided that I really wanted to further my studies in French and then work in France (though I never did). Needing to go to college, I applied to Tube Investments for a place on their undergraduate scheme. I still don't know to this day how I did it, but somehow, I persuaded them to use me as a guinea pig for a new type of apprentice, not an undergaduate at all, but rather a commercial apprentice, one who would not study engineering and not go to university. I was to go to technical college and study French and Export. I tried to persuade them to sponsor me to go to Manchester to study tourism and French. I was not successful in that but I was successful in getting sponsorship. I had to sign up as an indentured apprentice, I had to go to college locally and I had to work during college holidays. I had to repay them if I left my employment before an agreed date. In return, I received a wage.

Wednesbury College of Commerce and Technology, Wood Green Site (we didn't use the word campus in those days) welcomed me at a time when the Turtles were still "Happy Together", The Monkees were singing "I'm A Believer" and Scott McKenzie was wearing flowers in his hair in San Francisco. Flower power had arrived. Students had rioted at the

A Young Man's Years

London School of Economics, French students had marched through Paris protesting about Vietnam. Che Guevara, although dead, was a rallying icon for disenchanted student youth. Woodstock had changed the world.

I wasn't at university, I wasn't living away from home but I was a student and I had grown my hair to fit my new role.

I approached this new opportunity very positively and was rather proud of myself. Most fellow students received a grant from their local education department. I received a wage and it was paid into my own bank account every month. I lived the life of a student but had a bit more money. My fellow students were made up of other lads and girls from the surrounding Midlands and Shropshire plus some from far afield plus a number of Nigerians, sponsored by their government.

We tended to fall into two groups. The Nigerians stuck to their own kind, came every day in a suit and tie and demanded input or book knowledge as they called it. They expected the syllabus, no more and no less. They expected to have knowledge put into them by the teaching staff. In every way they were easy model students and they were very serious.

A Young Man's Years

The white students were generally scruffy and long haired. Whilst we knew we had to get through the syllabus, we wanted to debate, question, criticise, reason and argue. For us, education included fun and learning came from the experience of interaction with each other in the context of the subject in question.

The Nigerians wanted to know what to learn to pass an exam. They were rote learners. We wanted to know why and how, the what if's and the maybe's.

This was Enoch Powell's Britain yet there was no racial tension, no falling out. Both groups simply accepted that they were different and got on with life without upsetting the other.

We were all studying HND Business Studies (Higher National Diploma). Previously at Tube Investments, if you were an apprentice you only got day release. This together with night school enabled you to sit the Higher National Certificate (HNC) exams. HND was studied like a degree ie full time. We had college terms and long holidays (though in my case they were spent working). HND was regarded as a bottom end degree in a non academic subject. We studied the subjects that make up business – economics, accounting, commercial law, transport economics, business administration. In addition, I stayed on one night for French

A Young Man's Years

(Institute of Linguists) and Export studies (Institute of Export).

The course was three years long and after two, we had to choose a specialist subject from marketing, purchasing, personnel or accounting. I chose marketing mainly because none of the others interested me. Marketing offered the opportunity to study abstract subjects such as advertising and public relations at the same time learning new skills such as copywriting and product design. It turned out to be a good choice because the group I was with were the rebel group of the year and according to some the rebel group of the college's history. Our antics included going on strike, occupying part of a building and generally being awkward. Our marketing lecturer seemed to understand this behaviour and regard it as normal for people who would eventually work in the media, communication industry, public relations or advertising. This was our career path.

Being in marketing encouraged debate and argument. Subjects such as advertising had a basic framework but copyriting and ad creation is appreciated by the beholder. It isn't right or wrong or good or bad. It's right for some audiences, wrong for others; held in regard by some and criticised by others. This was not a world of 2+ 2=4. This was a world of well 2+2 can equal 4 but in certain

A Young Man's Years

circumstances, or looked at from a different perspective, can be interpretted differently.

Between college terms I would return to Tube Investments (TI). TI had many famous companies in its structure in those days. Accles and Pollock were world famous. The Japanese had claimed to make the worlds smallest tube, a fine syringe, I believe. A&P sent it back to them with one of theirs inside it! Any man was proud to work for such a company. I didn't need telling that TI was a blue chip company. If it could take the worlds smallest tube and make another to fit inside , that told me everything I needed to know. TI was world class and stood alongside other great Midlands manufacturers of the day – Round Oak, Stewarts and Lloyds, John Thompson to name but three. From it's Midlands factories, TI supplied the world.

I was employed by TI Stainless Tubes which was a company formed in 1963 from the merged stainless tube operations of Talbot Stead & Accles & Pollock. What we made is obvious. I worked at their Broadwell site in Oldbury and was one of many hundreds of workers. As an apprentice, I was required each holiday period, to work in a different area of the company. Heads of Department would report my achivements to Personnel and I think I did ok. I was "Apprentice Of The Year" on two occasions and won a cash prize with

A Young Man's Years

which I bought tools that I still own to this day. I truly "Rattled my bollocks in Accles & Pollock's" (apprentice rhyme). Some departments such as the Cost Office fascinated me. Others such as the technical drawing or Draughtsmans Office, I hated. I took the good with the bad and generally enjoyed what I did. Initially, I still had my scooter but then eventually bought my first car.

Due to the changing market for stainless tubing, TI built a bespoke factory at Green Lane in Walsall. It was there that they were to make the worlds largest "U" tubes for the nuclear power generation industry, particularly the American designed Pressure Water Reactor or PWR. At Walsall, I found my natural home in the Export Department and after finishing college worked there full time as an Export Clerk and as Assistant Technical Translator and Interpreter. France was a huge market so French tenders were coming in all the time. My job was to translate them. Desktop computers still did not exist so this was a hand writing process with finished sheets being given to the typing pool to type up for the attention of my boss Tim. Tender responses were done in the same way.

Tim was a large, rotund and jolly bachelor man. As much as I was striving to the future, with my head lost in the clouds, Tim, though probably only ten or so years older than me,

A Young Man's Years

was steeped in tradition with both feet firmly planted on terra firma. He smoked a pipe, collected stamps and belonged to the Civil Defence Association. Although an intellectual man, his work ethic was just the same as Jimmy the labourer. Work hard, earn your keep, do at least as much as expected and then a bit more for good measure – oh, and expect nothing in return other than job security and fair pay.

Tim and I got on well. I respected him and I think it was reciprocated. Our friendship continues to this day. I passed my HND. The Institute of Export had ceased offering examinations in Wednesdbury College so that had died a natural death. I passed the Institute of Linguists though not to the point of having letters after my name because to do so would have meant travelling to a college in Birmingham to complete it and I had somehow never got around to it. I passed my specialsim, the Institite of Marketing. This later became chartered and thus I became an MCIM.

I was pretty pleased with myself but disappointed with my fathers reaction. My brother had finished university to become a teacher as he had studied for a teaching certificate. His degree was to follow later in life. When I told my father of my passes at HND, Linguists and Marketing, he said "Well what are you now?" I said that I wasn't any

A Young Man's Years

one thing in particular. He said "Well what was the point". Today, you would simply study International Marketing and get a degree. In those days such courses did not exist.

During the time that I was at college in term time and TI in holiday time, two things happened which were to alter my life. I met my wife, Jill and I bought my first guitar, a classical acoustic Suzuki!

I met Jill at TI. She worked in the Shipping Department as a Clerk. She prepared documentation for all product despatched from the factory wherever it might be going in the world. I worked in Export so I guess for some time she was handling documents that I had processed. I put them in the internal mail not knowing my future wife was opening them. The Export Department was then in the main office block. Shipping Department was an office in the large Goods Outwards area and dealt with the logistics infrastructure of transport by ship, plane and lorries. Terms like FOB (Free On Board), CIF (Carriage, Insurance, Freight) and C&F (Carriage and Freight) were everyday terms. Obviously, road transport was involved in every despatch and lorry drivers must have been turning up all day and every day.

A Young Man's Years

Late one day a French driver arrived to collect tubing for a large French PWR project which we called "Creusot Loire".

(Much later in my life (1984) the Paris commercial court ordered the liquidation of Creusot-Loire, France's largest privately owned engineering conglomerate. The group's companies, had run up debts of more than $633 million and it was the biggest industrial bankruptcy in French history).

No one had a clue what he was on about and he spoke not a word of English. Shipping called on the interpretting skills of the Export Dept. The Interpretter was away and as such I was sent down to deal with him.

Although I had studied French to such a high level, it was all in a school environment. I had had one trip to France to study and that was for only one week! This bloke was the French equivalent of a Geordie and I hadn't a clue what he was talking about. I had to get him to write down what he was saying. Unfortunately he wrote as he spoke and in the same dialect. In simple terms, if he wrote "What are you called?" he would write it something like "Wot r u corled?" I felt very uncomfortable, as though I were a fraud. Eventually I resolved the situation but it took a while. I also met my wife to be!

All white collar functions on the site were eventually consolidated into the new office

A Young Man's Years

block. My wife to be was transferred into the same building as me. She was a small mini skirted beauty and I fell head over heels. I told her that I was going to marry her even though she was then engaged to someone else. I remember I fell into an office planter at the time. I was recently out of a long term relationship. Eventually she succumbed and we were married in Tettenhall in 1974.

We still worked together when we married though following to a fall off in orders due to the procrastination of the then labour government and their refusal to commit to a nuclear power programme, TI announced that the site was closing. As we had bought our first house in Shropshire, relocation was not an option. My boss Tim moved on to Chesterfield and sadly I didn't.

During this time, I was taking guitar lessons, classical guitar lessons. I was heavily into Donovan, Roy Harper and Caravan. I switched to steel stringed folk guitar and discovered Nigel Mazlyn Jones who in turn introduced me to the music of Michael Chapman and Roy Harper.

Nigel became a lifelong friend and I became a lifelong fan. He introduced me to various guitar tunings and guitar tablature. Tablature opened up the guitar fretboard and I began to pick out melodies and more importantly to be

A Young Man's Years

able to write them down so that I could refer to them in the future. I then began to write songs. In those early 1970's, I belonged to a generation that thought it could change the world. We had thrown off the shackles of the post war years, we had learned the lessons of the past. We could change the world with peace, love and music (and flowers). My early songs reflected this.

All this should have sat somewhat uncomfortably alongside a normal everyday job, a mortgage and all the other traditional things in life but somehow it worked. I found it easy to write protest songs against the system, smoke a joint and then go to work in a suit. It seems odd now but at the time, it was how it was for most of my generation. Yes, we had lived through the swinging sixties, yes to some extent we had created a sea of change. I felt like a revolutionary (even in a suit) and yet the changes we were able to achieve, whilst seemingly huge at the time are with hindsight, quite tiny and on many fronts have failed miserably through time. I guess that is how society evolves, slowly over a period of time but in a seemingly big way at particular points in time, as one lives through them. The subsequent withdrawl from Vietnam and eventually, the downing of the Berlin wall were in no small part due to the wave of protest from and by the people and count

A Young Man's Years

amongst the successes that can be traced back to my generations youth.

Against these huge successes are the failures in Africa, a continent still suffering under development, crop failure and repeated humanitarian crises; issues that I remember as a boy: the failure in the world's ability to co exist, Christian with Muslim, China with Tibet: the greed and self serving nature of Western government and the failure in Britain, one of the world's leading economies, to have a government that serves its people rather than its elected self. Hard to believe that in the years 2000 onwards in Britain, many pensioners live in poverty, the family unit is at risk of extinction, underage childbirth leads the world, young people cannot find or afford housing. The rich still get richer, the poor, poorer. The south east is still the focus of the UK and the rest of England is subjugated to London priorities. The Welsh have their Assembly and the Scots are pursuing independence. Each layer of public servant put more snouts in the trough to be fed by honest people trying to live their normal lives.

My friend Nigel saw all this coming and went on to work in Jersey with animals and it was many years later that I caught up with him, ironically through a visit to see Michael Chapman in concert in Lichfield. We were both examining the porcelain (as men do) when he

A Young Man's Years

told me that Nigel was back in England and living (quite reclusively) in Cornwall. Eventually, I tracked him down but by this time we had sadly lived a further twenty years of our lives.

Nigel sang at my wedding to Jill. He wrote a song just for the occasion. He was quite a celebrity in the local folk scene and folk was fashionable in those days. He made the front page of the local newspaper, the Express and Star. Jill and I were somewhere in the distant background! Jill got married in white and so did I. My suit was an off white with brown and cream shoes and shoulder length hair. We were married at St Michaels and All Angels, Lower Green, Tettenhall. A church wedding was the proper way to do things then. Registry Offices were then seen as indicating something was not quite right, a pregnant bride perhaps. Every mother dreamed of their daughter being married in white, in church and I am sure Jill's mom was no exception. Whether my mum expected her son to be married in white I do not know! She always knew Jill & I would marry and she was rarely wrong.

Passenger flight, quite undeveloped by today's standards, meant we could honeymoon

A Young Man's Years

abroad. I wanted to go to the Isle of Sky with Ned, my alsation/whippet dog.

We went to Lloret de Mar in Spain. It was warmer there in October!

"Three Minute Wonder"

> *The one-man band exists, in all its uniqueness and independence, as a most elusive yet persistent musical tradition. As a category of musicianship it transcends cultural and geographic boundaries, spans stylistic limits, and defies conventional notions of technique and instrumentation. Defined simply as a single musician playing more than one instrument at the same time, it is an ensemble limited only by the mechanical capabilities and imaginative inventiveness of its creator, and despite its generally accepted status as an isolated novelty, it is a phenomenon with some identifiable historical continuity - Hal Rammel, 1990*

It was August 7th, 2006 and I was on my way to London. I had left around 7.30am and needed to be in London at 1.30pm for an afternoon recording session which was to run until 6pm. The engagement was to record the soundtrack for a Channel 4 TV programme. The programme was called The Busker Symphony and was to be a contribution to the Three Minute Wonder series.

Three Minute Wonder was devised by Channel 4 as a medium to broadcast first time directors' three-minute TV programmes in the middle of the channel's weekday prime time schedule. Such first-time directors and producers were able to put their work in front of a large TV audience. The series was part of Channel 4's 4Talent initiative to help new talent break into the very competitive UK television industry. The series was broadcast at 7.55pm, weekday evenings, following the Channel 4 news. The

"Three Minute Wonder"

series comprehensively harvested the best of creative ideas from the history of the bicycle to Britain's last cinema organist, from the life history of Patrick Duffy (of TV's Dallas fame), to recycling.

I was to be working for Triplestop Films. They had been commissioned to produce a series of four mini documentaries on the many and varied facets of busking, good and bad. I had two sessions booked with them, one for sound recording, one for filming.

It was to Din Sound Studio in Cable Street, London E1 that I was now heading. I had limited knowledge of where I was going so had allowed plenty of time to get there. I had cleared the M6 north of Birmingham and the infamous Spaghetti Junction long before any traffic had built up. I was now on the M6 south of Birmingham heading for the M1. It was a grand day and I had both sunroofs open in my Renault Scenic. Behind me, I had removed the rear seats and was loaded with the various parephernalia of a One Man Band. Julie, the producer at Triplestop had hedged her bets and told me simply to bring everything. In that I knew we would eventually be on the street, I had limited my load to acoustic kit only and thus left my sack truck mounted digital option at home. Behind me was my "back rig" namely

"Three Minute Wonder"

a drum, tambourine & cymbals all mounted on an ex army rucksack frame. My second One Man Band, a "floor rig" revolved around a leather suitcase bass and washboard. In a stage setting, I often use these two together but for troubador work, the "back rig" facillitates mobility, critical at carnivals, street fairs and festivals. In addition to the "rigs" was my banjolele (in case they wanted any George Formby stuff), 12 string guitar, 6 string guitar, mandolin and my mouth truss (the mouth truss provides for harmonica, kazoo, whistles etc). All of this stuff merrily jangled in the back as I cruised along at a steady 60mph.

I have found as I grow older that I tend to drive slower than I used to. My wife reckons I am a danger to others mainly because I tend to lose myself in music. The car was equipped with a six stack CD player so I always carried a varied selection – Raymond Froggatt, Bushbury's, Nigel Mazlyn Jones, Downliners Sect, Penguin Café Orchestra and Woody's One Man Band would be a typical choice. A CD of my own usually features because it enables me to learn lyrics of my own songs as I drive from gig to gig. Cruising along, windows open, I was lost in "Tune For A Found Harmonium" by Penguin Café Orchestra. My mind drifted to childhood as I remembered early musical influences. "Singing The Blues" by Tommy

"Three Minute Wonder"

Steele (nee Hicks) was always one of my favourites and I recalled that I would sing it in the playground at Ettingshall Primary School with my friend Robert Harrop.

My childhood seemed to be filled with music, most of it from school. If I wasn't staying for school dinners, I would go to my nans for lunch. She was a true "black country wench" and always had particular days for doing particular household chores. One of my favourites was Friday.

"Hello nan" I would say as I walked in through her verandah. Nans verndah was long and thin. In school holidays it was a battlefied for my toy cowboys and indians but for her it doubled as a greenhouse and the smell of tomato plants assaulted the nostrils as you entered.

"Hello cock" she would say.

What have you done this morning nan?"

"I've 'ad a bloody good ferk in th'esshole" which meant " I have cleaned out the fire grate!"

Nans fire grate was big. It took up half the wall and had doors and heating cupboards as well as the open fire itself. It was black, the black of shiny coal. She would black it with some

"Three Minute Wonder"

strange compound simply called "blacking" which she applied to an old rag. She would of course get it all over her which was why whitening the doorstep was done on another day! On the top of nans fire range was a long black shelf. On there were her brasses. Later in life, I was to learn the her nub end Woodbines and Park Drive cigarettes would end up in a small brass jug on that shelf (perfect raw material for roll ups). Meals would take hours to cook and of course everything was freshly dug from her garden or bought from Bilston High Street that day. I remember one day she bought an eel. It had lay in the fishmongers van all the way from Grimsby. It had then lay on his marbled display counter in Bilston High Street when my nan saw it. Thinking it would provide a fine meal, she bought it. It lay in her shopping bag wrapped in newspaper as she returned home. It was an old leather bag. Shopping bags lasted a lifetime then. Plastic carrier bags had not yet been invented. Unwrapped, the eel then lay on the wooden draining board. She armed herself with a big knife to chop off its head and it lay there no more. I entered from the verandah to witness her chasing the eel around the kitchen swiping at it's head at every opportunity. Eventually she got it but even without it's head it carried on.

"Three Minute Wonder"

Nan would hum and sing to herself as she worked. Whilst I was there for my lunch (we called it dinner) we would often listen to the wireless (radio). I don't know why it was called a wireless because it was plugged into the wall. Not the square pinned plugs of today but the old fashioned round plugs. I understand the term wireless refers to the fact that the signals it receives are not sent via a wire or cable as was the case with telegraphy. In those days we would listen to the BBC Light Programme. This was the predeccessor of todays Radio 1 and 2. Appropriately named, "Workers Playtime" was broadcast during working break hours ie lunchtime. I think it was for about half an hour, three times a week. First broadcast on BBC's Home Service as part of the war effort in 1941, it was switched to the Light Programme in 1957 and continued until 1964. From George Formby to the Beatles, it entertained the masses and introduced me to lifelong fascination with the old music hall and variety stars – Ken Dodd, Charlie Chester, Arthur Askey to name but three. It was shrouded in secrecy, befitting its wartime birth and was a touring show broadcast from a "factory canteen somewhere in Britain" and always finished with the saying "Good luck, all workers". I remember that if I was ever off school poorly, my mom would listen to "Music While You Work" (MWYW), another wartime legacy that lasted through my

"Three Minute Wonder"

childhood. Lasting through to 1967, MWYW was unique in that it's makers were specifically tasked to be repetetive and even tempo'd. Slow music and waltzes were banned. The music had to mimic the rhythms of the factory floor and encourage repetition. Melodies had to be "whistleable" and artistic licence, music sublties and tempo variation was discouraged. One Man Bands would have gone down well but I guess there were none to found on recordings at the time.

When my nan had fed and watered me, she would pack me off to school. She would always ensure I was properly attired. In the winter, she would always wrap my scarf around my face. "Doh yow gerra draft on yower face. Yow'll get lockjaw".

All these years later, the very thought mortified me and I quickly shut the car windows. There was no way today I could risk lockjaw. I am sure it is an old womans tale but you never know. You don't hear of these sorts of ailments today, nor do you see the post war sights that us children of the 1950's saw. Not just those that could be related to the war but illnesses and ailments attributable to hardship, foul air, poor sanitation and poor nutrition. I remember my nans best friend Mrs P..... We would often meet her on the way to Bilston town. She had some

"Three Minute Wonder"

sort of flesh eating illness because it seemed that half her face was missing. As a child she terrified me, poor woman. In spite of such ailments, we didn't suffer from obesity and all our food was fresh. We might sit in the gutter to eat our "doorsteps" (rough cut sandwiches), but our immunity was at a far higher threshold than today.

Anyway, back to lockjaw. I moved my bottom jaw from side to side and vigorously rubbed my face to ensure that the draught had not taken it's toll. I seemed ok! For reasons unknown, I had been offered a number of TV jobs in recent times. Initially I had become very excited to receive eMails and telephone calls from representatives of famous broadcasters on both terrestial and satellite TV stations. I had received a number of approaches from people with famous and impressive addresses. Not one had come to anything. I had learned that TV personnel are like a rash. When they want you they are all over you. You fight to keep your breath such is the onslaught. Just as quickly as they make up their mind, they change it. At that point, you, the excited one, drop from their line of vision. They have no idea of the impact they have made on your life. You have seen the equivalent of a lottery win come within a whisker of your grasp. As an entertainer, you have almost put something on your CV that

"Three Minute Wonder"

could change your life – but not quite made it. A TV offer that comes to nothing is like a missed goal. It is worth nothing.

I had become exhaused and frustrated with the missed opportunities when I received an eMail from Julie Clare, Producer at Triplestop Films Ltd.

I found your website and was intrigued. We are a company called Triplestop Films and are making 4 low budget short documentaries for Channel 4's 3 Minute Wonder strand - those little shorts after their evening news.
Ours is entitled, The Busker Symphony and looks at the experience of busking from various perspectives. The films are all being set to original music being composed by our RTS Award Nominated Director/Composer Benjamin Till.
For the 1st of the 4 films we are looking for a one man band to feature at the start and end of the piece. If there's any chance you might be interested, could you give me a call on the number below - or give me a number where I can contact you.

I'd be very grateful.

I had dutifully sent off my CD's for Julie's consideration and thought little more of it. I presumed, like all the others it would all come to nothing. I didn't mind sending out CD's as I took the view that something might crop up in the future. A few exchanges ensued re fees and possible dates.

On August 3rd, an eMail "Letter of Engagement" was received. I was astounded and my faith in TV producers was suddenly

"Three Minute Wonder"

restored. Four days later, here I was en route to London to record in a proper recording studio. I say proper because like many entertainers I too have my home recording studio. It's so easy today. Also in a former musical format with the Unicorn Folk Group, I had been a group member when we recorded a cassette tape in someone's house. To be fair, he was a real recording engineer but the location was still not a proper studio.

I had "GOOGLED" DinSound and found that it was located right by the River Thames. Its list of clients meant nothing to me. At my age, modern artists mostly pass me by unnoticed. However there were two names that impressed me. Firstly there was the BBC Children in Need (of Terry Wogan fame). More importantly, there was "THE POGUES".

THE POGUES had been around since 1982 and were originally called Pogue Mahone (a Gaelic term which apparently means Kiss My Arse). A name like that makes a statement! Their blend of original, old time and cover songs all set in the tradition of Irish music was a winner in the folk rock world that I had grown out of. Add to that a heavy dose of punk, fast beats and plenty of attitude and they were always destined for the world stage. I believe that it was the BBC who demanded that their name was changed. It

"Three Minute Wonder"

was shortened to The Pogues and they were the wild men of folk and pop. I couldn't ask for more (except Abbey Road perhaps!!).

The sun was up and the M6 miles flew by. My early morning lavatorial routine was unsettled by the early rise so I needed to stop and use the facilities. I pulled into the next services. It was now around 10am and I was making good time. I considered the safety of my equipment as it was on full view in the car. However, when considering the alternative, I decided that I had no choice. The pressure on my sphincter was quite unbearable as though a herd of cows was trying to break loose. I parked as near to the service entrance as possible and made my way in. There was the usual gauntlet of "street vendors" impeding my entrance as I rushed to find the facilities. This was not the loo of the year but I didn't care as I ripped my trousers open. I remembered an identical situation in Tenerife when my new digital camera, bought that holiday, flew from my belt and down the pan. Strangely enough, once extricated it from the water it continued to work fine. The first few photos were a little wet looking but otherwise it was ok.

Sitting on the pan and releasing one's bowel muscles rates as one of the most pleasurable experiences I know. The world is instantly a

"Three Minute Wonder"

better place and life again seems worth living. Sadly, all too soon, the pleasure is gone and the need to button up and go takes precedence. Suddenly my mobile rang:

"Woody"
"Yes"
"Julie here, where are you". I wondered how to answer this one. I could have said "I'm sat on the pan in the services on the M6, just about to wipe my backside". I didn't.
"Oh hi Julie, I'm on the M6 near the M1" I said hoping the bloke in the next cubicle wouldn't fart again.
"Slight change of plan Paul. The BBC have booked DinSound this afternoon to record Radio 2's Folk Guitarist of the Year"
"Thanks a lot BBC, thanks a lot Mike Harding, and thanks a lot whoever you are" I thought.
"Oh that's ok Julie" said I instead (unconvincingly).
"Your slot has been moved to 6pm 'till 10pm. Is that ok?"
"Oh that's fine Julie, even better" said I dishonestly. I now had eight hours to complete a drive which even at my speed would only take two hours.
"Means I can take a leisurely drive! See you later".

"Three Minute Wonder"

Just then the bloke in the next cubicle flushed. I hope I had disconnected Julie before she heard.

"Well, what do I do now" thought I. To drive home and back to this point could have taken three hours. To drive on to London would take two. I would be there by 1pm at the latest, five hours early. I decided to press on. Better to be early than late.

I 'phoned home to explain my circumstances and then set off again.

"I could have had another two hours in bed" I thought. I had been up and away by 7.30am. Though it may seem improbable, it reminded me of my student days. Most students would lie in bed until at least 10am. Not me. I had to take my turn in the paper shop which my mom & dad ran. If I was not downstairs by 5.30am, with the shop open, all lights on and ready to serve, Mr G…….. would tap on the drainpipe with his penny coin. It was February 1971 when Britain's coinage was decimalized. Pre that date it was half crowns, thruppences, sixpences or shillings etc known simply as "pounds, shillings and pence". I remember that there were 12 pence in a shilling and twenty shillings in a pound. Therefore there were 240 pennies in a pound. After decimalization, the pound remained but now it comprised only 100

"Three Minute Wonder"

pennies. No wonder everything went up in price. It was with one of these said pre decimal pennies that Mr. G would tap monotonously on the drainpipe. If I didn't hear it my dad would wake me. I then felt guilty because his sleep had been disrupted. That entire disturbance for a Daily Mirror!!

Life at 5.30am is different to the rest of the day. The world is waking. Most people are still asleep in bed but some are already up and out. In the winter, it is dark, still night in fact. I remember one day that a customer came in and said they thought they had seen a body on the "village" green. When my dad came down, I left him to cover the shop and went to investigate. Sure enough, I found a body. A man on his way to work, complete with sandwiches for the day, had simply keeled over and died. Sadly some years later, at about the same time of the day, whilst walking the dog before he went to work, my dad died in the same way. Just fell over in the street, all very quick and tidy. The dog sat guarding him as dogs do.

It was whilst I was at the newsagent, as a student, that my musical endeavors began. I had traded my Suzuki classical for a steel strung Yamaha. I had received some lessons

"Three Minute Wonder"

from my friend to be, Mazlyn Jones and I had begun writing lyrics and picking out melody.

The earliest photographic record of me and a guitar are in the rear garden of that newsagents shop (1970) and then with Ned, my Alsatian whippet (1972).

Here now, all those years later, I was travelling to a real recording studio to record for a programme to be broadcast on a national TV station.

I got to London about 1am. Firstly I followed the signs to dockland and ended up literally alongside the Thames. The studio was nearby and was easily found. It was literally a stones

"Three Minute Wonder"

throw from the river and Julie's description of it had been accurate –
" I should warn you it's a unique and ramshackle building"

She did add " but houses many creative people".

The studio was unique. I think it was the only one to be left un-restored following the Blitz. "Ramshackle" did not begin to describe the desolation that stood before me. Clearly it was some sort of ancient riverside warehouse. The courtyard was cobbled and it looked a fairly jaded area with lots of litter blowing about. I noticed a poster on the wall advertising a local gay club either in or near to the building. I decided to have a kip in the car whilst I waited (with the doors locked in case the club was nearby). The car was fully loaded so I couldn't risk leaving it. Julie had asked me to bring pretty much everything except the kitchen sink :

"We'd like you to bring your acoustic set-up plus any other instruments you think might be useful! I understand your acoustic set-up to be: Old leather suitcase used as a drum, on top is washboard activated by same drum pedal, cymbal, bicycle bell, tin mug, bottle tops, cow bell, tea pot and jug. Mouth truss has siren, kazoo, harmonica, whistle. Also 12 string guitar, mandolin, 6 string guitar, banjolele uke".

I had all this with me and more!

"Three Minute Wonder"

Eventually, I saw a couple of young musicians leaving the building and guessed they were the Radio 2 guys, the "Young Guitarist of the Year" and his mate. Julie's production assistant arrived and together with studio staff we began taking all my kit inside and upwards. The place was cavernous with an antiquated lift. We were somewhere in the higher reaches at the end of a long corridor. Everything was fairly anonymous and there was none of the "showbiz" that I expected. At that point it was rather a let down. I hadn't yet sampled the professionalism of the studio which of course is what counts. All my kit was finally levered into a tiny recording studio. Every inch of wall seemed to have cables, wires and spare leads hanging there from. Adjacent to the studio was the sound recordist's room which of course was behind glass and completely out of my hearing except for a communication speaker in the studio linked to his microphone. I set up my kit much to the amusement of all concerned after which I was asked to demo what I did to enable sound checks. I seemed to end up surrounded by about five microphones all focusing on different parts of my OMB rig and each obviously going separately into the mixing desk. Benjamin Till, the Director/Composer was there and I was surprised at his youth. He had written the score and lyrics that I was to

"Three Minute Wonder"

perform. Called simply "The Busker Symphony" it read :

"A thousand decibels of endless sights and sounds, you call it hell
A grim cacophony of car alarms and sirens beeps and shrieks and yells
I disagree
So listen carefully and then you'll hear a hundred melodies
This is the city symphony"

The Symphony was to be performed in the key of C. As I usually play in Drop D tuning this was not one of my favourite keys to play or sing in but Ben was very particular about how he wanted it to sound. In the studio of course, I could only hear what I was doing. The whole thing took about 5 hours. Although I performed as a One Man Band, Ben insisted on me adding a mandolin fill and a teapot solo! Studying it later on the studio computer, I was amazed at the level of technology in this little set of rooms.

What an experience it was – and there was more to come. I drove home on a high not having wanted the day to end.

My next day in London was for filming. I received my Call Sheet which detailed the affairs of the day :

"Three Minute Wonder"

THE BUSKER SYMPHONY
Call Sheet

Date:	25/08/06
Director:	Ben Till
Producer:	Julie Clare
Shoot Day:	1
Camera:	Vic Marwaha
Production Manager:	Katharine Simkins
Crew Call:	06.40
Camera Assistant:	Jonathan Velardi
Health & Safety:	Cenay Said
Weather:	Light rain, max.temp 20c
Runners:	Nez & Jes
Sunrise:	06.00
Sunset:	20:02
7am	Practice wheelchair shot
8am	Tracking shot
	Both above in Sclater Street

Telephone numbers were of course included for everyone and the Call Sheet detail continued to include other filming done on the day for further programmes in the series.

I turned up on the day and found the location easily. 7am was an ungodly hour and I had left before 5 in the morning. Sclater Street was just off Brick Lane. As an outsiders to London, that meant nothing to me except that I think it was somewhere near Petticoat Lane.

"Three Minute Wonder"

Parking provision had been made with some sort of "grease the palm" arrangement. Ben was there as was Julie and the rest of the crew. It was straight down to business as we each set ourselves up for the shoot.

I was positioned near some graffiti and fly posters. The camera was to approach me in a sweep of the street, trained on the wall where I would be stood at some point. Having passed me, I was then to leg it up the road and appear again with another OMB rig. For the first part of the shoot it was my back rig, for the second part my suitcase bass, washboard and teapot would feature. Filming was done with the cameraman sat in a wheelchair that had been procured from somewhere. As the recording had been studio produced I was to mime or "lip sync" to use the modern terminology. Julie was to be my "cue

"Three Minute Wonder"

card" and the recording that had been done would be played from an mp3 plus speaker carried by one of the runners. I had often seen the term runner on film credits and learned on the day it means exactly what it says – run here, run there, fetch this, fetch that.

As I stood there whilst things were tried out, I marveled at Julie & Ben's choice of location and understood the extent of their skill. This was a nondescript street, perhaps the sort of street you wouldn't want to be alone on at night. To the film maker it was a palette of opportunity. Just where I stood, the walls were bedecked with endless visual opportunity. These were the sort of sights we all see every day and walk past yet they had seen them in a completely different light. It made me realize how much sensory information we screen out. They simply opened their senses to what is in front of us all every day. Julie, particularly, seemed to have an encyclopedic knowledge of the area and proved it many times later that day.

Julie had been responsible for my appearance. She wanted the English look and my deerstalker won the day (thanks again to the Downliners Sect all those years previously). Ben had found an old tail coat which combined with denim jeans and a white shirt with folded back cuffs delivered the look that Julie wanted.

"Three Minute Wonder"

(If you look carefully above, you can see the camera crew traveling by wheelchair).

"Three Minute Wonder"

"Three Minute Wonder"

At the other end of the street, I was to reappear with my teapot and suitcase bass on sack truck.

The credits for the soundtrack were given as "**Woody's One Man Band and the Sounds Of The Streets Of London**" and filming was undertaken accordingly.

The film started down the street with the camera trained to the wall against which I was stood. The camera maintained its angle whereby at some time I came into its line of vision along with the fly posters and graffiti. The Symphony faded in and out as the camera approached and then passed. As it then traveled along it took in the sights and sounds of the street. Everyday objects such as street debris and rubbish featured both in sight and sound.

Out of camera range, I ran up the street and reappeared as per the above shot, with my suitcase bass, washboard and teapot. We did about three takes and then a few stills in neigbouring streets and then it was all over. The finished article was broadcast on April 2nd, 2007. I think most of my friends thought that it had never happened at all such was the time between filming and public viewing.

"Three Minute Wonder"

I couldn't believe that the broadcast clashed with a major story line on Britain's most popular soap "Coronation Street". Instead of feeling cheated, I decided to use the opportunity to write my song "Is She Guilty" as mentioned before.

Mid Life Crisis

Nothing prepares a man for mid his mid life crisis. Suddenly the biological drive has gone. Children are in their teenage years and their heads full of what were once one's own young dreams. For women it is easier in that there is an acknowledged mid life change. For men, nothing! You have reached the time, wherever you are in your career, a point at which it is as good as it gets. From here on it is downhill. Younger, more talented upstarts are nipping at your heels and day to day life can become quite wearisome. It was about this time, whilst in the Unicorn Folk Group, that I wrote a song entitled "Mid Life Crisis" :

>His hair it still hangs long but now its grey
>And its thinning on the top
>And his jeans are just too tight
>And his belly hangs a little out the top
>The badge for CND is gone, its absence makes him smart
>Though he no longer shouts it out, its still there in his heart
>He's in his mid life crisis
>Was he always in a crisis from the start.

Over the years, so many people have come up to me and expressed how they identify with this song. It was written on the M42. As is oft on Britain's motorways, it was at a standstill. It was March 1996 and I was in the inside lane, stationary, playing my harmonica at the wheel. In the middle lane was a man about

Mid Life Crisis

my age but with a grey pony tail, his "sales rep" jacket hanging from a coat hanger in the back. In my mind, I juxtaposed us both and the song was the result.

Women have a predefined expectation of when the "change" will start. I knew when my mother had started. There were no more monthly "sheet rags" on the fireguard drying. Women of my generation were the first to experience the benefits of shop bought sanitary towels and of course insert products. My mother's generation, (those women who were childbearing in the 1950's), simply recycled old bed sheets. My mom would rip them into tea towel sized sections and they would serve their new purpose thereafter. I guess in many ways, such items were part of the reason that everything needed to be boiled. She would dry them in front of the fire whilst she had a cup of tea or Camp coffee (chicory & coffee essence). I was usually seconded into the knitting routine, holding a skein of wool which she had bought cheap or an expired woolen sweater about to enter a new life of rework as a reworked, re knitted smaller item. I had to hold my arms out straight pulling out the skein into a flat oval. She would then roll the wool into a ball. Whilst doing this I would stare into the flickering flames of the fire, my

Mid Life Crisis

imagination running wild; my mother's rags puffing steam from the heat.

My mother was always talking about the "change". She was a martyr to it and constantly reminded the whole family how lucky they were that she had dealt with it so well. I don't know if my dad had a change in life. His mood rarely changed and he always seemed the same. Having come from a generation that had nothing, he was grateful for his lot and never expected more. My mother did expect more and it was she who drove the family to bigger and better things. It was always she who wanted to move, to buy a business, to buy a bigger car. Not that she expected any of it for nothing; she and my dad had a work ethic that meant nothing came without long hours and hard graft and my mother was a grafter.

One expectation that came from their hard work was that their children would have a better life than they did and I think in most if not all cases, we did. However one outcome of that was the material world with its envy & greed. My generation has seen huge technological and social change. Not only has man walked on the moon, invented household computers and developed mass passenger air travel, but expectations of

Mid Life Crisis

healthcare, housing and social care have increased too. The result is today's nanny state. Fathers now get paternity leave, victims get counselling, soldiers join up for a career not expecting to go to war, prisoners have rights (more than their victims) and we have invented political correctness. Today's world is crammed with 'ism's - ageism, sexism, racism to name but three.

One early outcome of these changes to my generation is that men were now afforded the right to a mid life crisis. My dad had been too busy feeding and clothing us kids. Unlike him, I had the luxury to indulge myself. I don't know when it started really and I'm not sure if and when it ever ended. I think it was about 1993 when for the first time in my life I found myself unemployed, my friends started dying, first or even second generation pets were meeting their maker, girls stopped noticing me, hair started thinning, trousers went up a size, cars became sensible, pensions became interesting, life insurance a bargain not to be missed, the future a worry and absence of savings a concern.

Following the loss of employment at Tube Investments in the early 1970's, I had somehow ended up in the toilet and kitchen cleaning industry. Whilst that may seem a

Mid Life Crisis

world apart from engineering, there is a thread of common ground – marketing. That is what I was trained to do and that is what I went to do in the toilet cleaning industry. I used all my transferable skills without knowing that's what they were and at the same time learned about selling, sales training and well – cleaning lavatories and commercial kitchens. The cleanest lavatory I ever went in was in a Nottinghamshire mine: the dirtiest kitchen – a London hospital. I extricated solidified rats from cooker ranges and learned the technicalities of mass murder of cockroach infestations. I learned how to clean the insides of commercial extraction units and the drains of urinals. I also met the man that was to be my best friend – Doug.

Loving the world of hygiene I moved on to expand my knowledge in the cleaning and laundry industry. From 1974 to 1988, Jill and I ran our own textile rental business providing and washing rental workwear to local industry. It was a happy period of our life but not without financial pressure. Doug meanwhile had gone on to form his own business too and though he asked me to join him, our friendship was never to be polluted by business differences. When Jill & I were seduced by the predatory approach of a large PLC, we sold up, pretty much without much

Mid Life Crisis

thought as to what to do thereafter. During the time of our business our two boys grew up, we built a house with our own fair hands. It took us 10 years all in all and we pretty much did it all. Electrical work, plumbing and glazing skills were bought in but the actual build was mostly done by ourselves and paid out of earned income. The house was a mile down a farm track and we had a large farm gate across our drive. People often want to "lock the world out". For us, our gate was a barrier to the world and we loved our years there. The kids grew up using the footings for trench warfare and the walls for mountaineering skills. Family life was as good as it got. At the foot of the garden was a half acre paddock. Our two donkeys, Primrose and Jemma lived there. We built them a Spanish style stable block complete with self closing saloon doors so they could come and go as they pleased. Their paddock was originally an orchard though over the years they ate the trees one by one. Their favourites were the damsons. They would chew the fruit and crunch the stones. They, like us, lived a happy life. The only blot on their times were the farrier visits. He was a bit rough with them mainly because he had to be. They didn't like him and he was none too keen either. I think they were the only donkeys he looked after. Horses were obviously far easier.

One of my hobbies included driving our two donkeys. The above photograph was taken in 1987 with Simon and Primrose at the Newport (Salop) Boxing Day Parade. Both donkeys were taught to be very good "drivers". We once tried them in tandem but it was a nightmarish experience as the leading donkey was out of shafts and could turn 180 degrees to try to see the one behind. Working with them along the local lanes and tracks of Newport in Shropshire was a wonderful experience. So many new things befell them at every trip – a puddle, an echo, paper blowing in the wind, traffic lights etc. I remember one Boxing Day Parade for a very

Mid Life Crisis

particular reason. We all made our way from the Smithfield Market to St Mary's St, Newport's cobbled street alongside the church. All carriages filed out from the market as special requirements had to be met. The leading horse for example, although a semi shire ie very big, was terrified of donkeys! We had to hide away somewhere in the middle until called out. We would then gallop up the road and turn right into the cobbled street. There, we would typically stand for 20 minutes or so being served mince pies and sherry. During this time, the animals would be feted and admired by the crowds that had assembled. Primrose always attracted a lot of attention. She (or Jemma, or both) was the only donkey in the parade and people always have a soft spot for donks! Being Boxing Day of course, she would be suitably dressed in glitter and baubles. Once I was told that Prim was ill because she was foaming at the mouth. She had in fact been given an extra strong mint by an admirer and unable to chew it, (because of her bridle) was sucking and foaming at the same time. Eventually we would "drive off", do a sharp turn up and along the High St. On this particular occasion as we trotted up the road the lights changed from green to red. Prim ground to a halt and no amount of persuasion would encourage her to move until the lights

Mid Life Crisis

changed to green. The crowds of course interpreted this as intelligence (I knew it was stubbornness) and she received a rousing cheer. Although usually the smallest in the parade she would easily overtake other carts and coaches, even up hill! At the top of the High St the parade would U turn and come back again to the beginning from which we would drive out into the countryside a few miles to a village pub. More mince pies and sherry then back to town for a bevy! The U turn could be problematical especially as on one occasion the leading horse saw Prim and hightailed uncontrollably off parade, ending up in its own paddock, far from any threatening donkey!

Two other memorable experiences spring to mind. One was an invite from the local supermarket to take our two donkeys in store to assist in their participation in a national Seville orange competition. We took the donkeys by horsebox into town after closing and then lead them by head collar into the store. It seemed very odd to be walking a field animal through the frozen foods and dairy product. The vegetable and fruit displays certainly caught their attention. They were photographed with the orange display and I recall that the store either won or did very well in the competition.

Mid Life Crisis

The second experience was with my mother in law. She loved to come out for a drive when visiting us and nothing could beat a gentle trot through the countryside on a pleasant summer's day. That is until we met water cannon shooting gallons of water a second across both the fields and the track we were on. The cannon moved just as we entered its reach and we were drenched. My mum had a thin cotton summers dress and instantly looked like an entrant to a pensioners "wet T shirt" competition. Primrose of course found the shower of water very refreshing and refused to move. We two, meanwhile, were pounded by bullet like slugs of high speed water. My mother in law talks of that day even now, many years on.

During this part of my life I also succeeded in becoming a 1st Dan black belt in Wado Ryu Karate. This took me about 7 years and many hours of training. My black belt was taken in London under the legislative eye of Vic Charles, 5th Dan, then world heavyweight champion (1986/7).

At the same time I joined the Unicorn Folk Group. Joining the group took me from being a backroom strummer to standing in front of an audience. Making music with others

Mid Life Crisis

taught me about timing and empathy. Holding an audience with music taught me about tonal variety or light and shade as one band member called it. The band provided the opportunity to do some solo spots and I found that I had a natural talent as a raconteur and entertainer. I never rose to the heights of being a good musician but I was adequate. Being a "folkie" meant I generally sang long story type songs. To this day, I find it difficult not to tell a story and almost impossible to keep to the three and a half minute rule. It was also during this time that I introduced a folk audience to the music of the Lancashire lad, George Formby!

After selling our business and without a proper plan, I somehow lost my way and suffered from loss of identity. The easiest way to encapsulate what I mean is that when in business, I was always introduced as "This is Paul. He and Jill own …." That became "This is Paul". I ended up working for the PLC that we had sold our business to and travelled the country on their behalf as a Director of Marketing and Development. As well as all their laundries, I found myself working on huge food sites such as Heinz (baked beans), Sara Lee (cakes), Smiths and Walkers (crisps). I was then headhunted by a competitor and found myself working in

Mid Life Crisis

Bradford, West Yorkshire. I use the phrase "found myself" because that really summed up how it was. There was no plan and I exercised little control over events. During this time, I regret to say that I was a weekend dad and husband. Eventually, it became too much and I chose to resign. I was pretty much at the top of my tree and expected to find work more local to my home in weeks if not days. The opposite proved to be the case.

Apart from being away from home, I loved working in Bradford. I loved the people and I loved the geography of the area. We even thought of moving there but sadly the company was shaky and it did not seem a sensible thing to do. Eventually it did close but that was not until 2007.

The staff at Bradford had a whip round and I decided to buy an electronic tuner for my guitar. I went to buy it the day before I left. As I sat in traffic, I noticed what appeared to be a music junk shop or second hand shop. Sitting there in my car, I thought I saw a banjolele or ukulele banjo hanging from the ceiling. It was impossible to park at that time to take a look so I recorded the shop name, intent on calling them before I left Bradford. I did just that and was told that yes indeed it was a banjolelele and that they had two. I

Mid Life Crisis

arranged to call in the next day, my last day in Bradford.

During the 1950's and '60's, I had grown up with the music and films of George Formby. George had passed his peak during my growing up, his main success years being pre 1945. After the war, a bit like Winston Churchill, he reminded people of the war years, years they wanted to forget so he tended to be seen and heard less on TV, radio and cinema. He found a whole new generation of fans in places like South Africa where he was recorded singing in the Africaan language. Although I didn't realize it at the time, George was a major influence on the generation to come; my generation. Few would quote him as an influence on the pop music to come yet early skifflers like Lonnie Donegan and Chas McDevitt had seen this man stand on stage and entertain thousands with his little ukulele. Those pre rock n roll years, mid '50's and before, my parents generation were entertained by the big bands and the crooners. George was one of few exceptions and the most successful and nationally known.

Other famous string players included Max Miller and Billy Uke Scott. A typical lunchtime at my nan's would include

Mid Life Crisis

"Workers Playtime" on which I think Billy was a regular. Like George, Billy was a superb player and sang (his own), novelty songs. His spot always ended with a display of his ukemanship and the words - 'And finally, to prove that melody can be played on the ukulele...' I also remember Tessie O'Shea and Gracie Fields.

George didn't croon, in fact he hadn't got a particularly good voice. He had a strong regional dialect (Lancashire) and acted daft. He was the loser that always won the girl and everyone loved him. He also played the ukulele which in time was replaced by a banjolele (ukulele banjo). The banjolele suited George's fast syncopated rhythm and had a sound that carried even in the midst of a full orchestra complete with brass section. George stood on the stage on his own, just him and his uke. He was acknowledged by the early skifflers and latterly by The Beatles. They wanted to stand on stage too and entertain. They knew it could be done, George had done it!

In Chas McDevitt's "Skiffle – The Definitive Inside Story" he writes :
"As far as I was concerned, George Formby was to blame, well, George Formby and his ukulele or, to be more precise, his ukulele-banjo. George Formby's films and records made in the late 1930's and wartime years, cut a swathe through all this romantic

Mid Life Crisis

candyfloss. As my peer group and I grew up, this string driven music found it's full expression in the skiffle music of the 1950's. We realized that music could be made quite easily and bright and cheerful music it was."

I entered the shop and there was my George Formby banjolele. I was a guitarist so I had no idea how to play it. The owner of the shop took it down and tuned it. It had a copper back and looked like a frying pan. His colleague took down the other instrument and together they launched into one song after another. On the counter was a piano accordion. A passer by, laden with two bags of heavy shopping and looking a bit like Harry Worth, came in the shop and asked if the piano accordion worked. Reassured that it did, he strapped it on and led my two performers in song after song. After about half an hour, he put the accordion back on the counter, thanked them and walked out.

Of course I bought the uke. That year, 1993, I joined the George Formby Appreciation Society which gave me the opportunity to appear on the stages of Blackpool Winter Gardens and the branch venues of village halls and British Legion Social Clubs.

After leaving Bradford, I found it very hard to find work. Being at the top of my tree I

Mid Life Crisis

really expected to be headhunted again, but I was not. I did a little consultancy work. Consultancy was the fashionable description for white collar people "between jobs". Through some work I did in the NHS I eventually landed a job with an Executive Agency of the Cabinet Office. It was based in Liverpool, in the Liver building. The Agency had advertised for specialists to account manage their activities in the component parts of the public sector – education, local government, central government, Ministry of Defence etc. One sector was the NHS. I was the only applicant with any NHS experience and although I had little, I had some so I got the job. I loved working for in Liverpool though I struggled to adapt to the public sector work ethic which was to do as little as was needed to get by. Certainly never do any more.

Prior to landing the Agency job, I had a heart attack, nothing serious but enough to put me in hospital for a week and then several weeks' recuperation (including a week in Cornwall with my old guitar teacher, Nigel Mazlyn Jones). It was a sign of my growing years, my stresses and the ups and downs of my working life. Jill and I had struggled financially without the sort of income I was used to and, work aside, I was running at

Mid Life Crisis

90mph with karate and the band. I have never been one to do anything lightheartedly, in fact I guess I am obsessive; I always strive to be my best.

The job in Liverpool put me into a working group of other ex private sector men, most with similar tales to mine. All of us were past our best year, graying or thinning hair with early signs of pot bellies. I realised that my experiences were not unique.

Working in Liverpool enabled me to explore Mathew Street, famous for the Beatles and it enabled me to take in the Liverpool music scene. My friends knew I was a "musician" and one night I was persuaded to sing and play with the Merseysippee Jazz Band. They were brilliant and more than covered my for limited experience.

Eventually, I was transferred to Oxford, seconded from Agency to a private sector partner company, as an Account Manager within the NHS. This was not exactly a joint venture but near enough for explanation purposes. I deeply missed my Liverpool colleagues and though I was working in the private sector, I was still paid at a low grade Civil Service rate.

Mid Life Crisis

Having been at the top of my tree, I resented this and when the opportunity arose to take on a directorship with a small but growing company operating laundry services within the NHS I seized the chance. This put me in charge of ex NHS facilities in Cornwall, Devon and Essex. Whilst enjoyable, I was again back into part time husband and father and trying to live a seven day domestic life in two days. The whirligig took its toll and due to under funding and over trading, the company struggled. Working away from home did have its plus sides. I would spend my evenings picking and strumming my guitar and ukulele and even write the odd song. Sadly there was little opportunity to perform them. I did seek out the occasional folk club and do a spot when I could but as I had no routine of time or geography it was not easy.

I had kept in touch with my old boss from Oxford. He was one of life's gentlemen, The last of a kind and he had made it clear that should an opportunity arise, I would be favourably considered. Such a job did arise and I was considered. I got it!

Oxford, second time around was much more fun, at least I was paid for the job I was doing. Again, much travel was involved and my

Mid Life Crisis

trusty Martin Backpacker and my little wooden uke were never far away.

When the parent company decided to sell their subsidiary, I was needed to re contract with new owners. The consequence of this was much more time spent in Oxford and possibly a relocation. I chose not to do this and found myself once more in the job market.

Most people of my generation remember where they were when Kennedy was assassinated in 1963. I don't. I remember that I was walking up Regent Street in Bilston in February, 1958 when I heard that Manchester United had crashed at Munich. I remember that I was in Bradford with friends when Princess Diana died in August, 1997. I remember that I was in the hills around Moffat in Scotland on the day that Diana was buried on September 6th, 1997.

I also remember being on the M42 near Warwick Services when I heard that Richard Walker had died in 1999. Being a folkie, I had long listened to Sunday Folk on BBC Radio Shropshire. The programme was presented by Richard Walker a local storyteller and lover of folk music. Richard had a fine radio voice and could talk his subject with wit and

Mid Life Crisis

intelligence. Richard Walker's show was a "must listen" every Sunday at 8pm. If that was not possible then a cassette recording was essential. His voice captivated me and being a storyteller, he was able to use his wordsmith skills across the air for two hours every week. I had missed the previous night's show but was now listening to my cassette as I sped along the M42 towards Oxford. I pushed it in and Genevieve Tudor's voice came on saying that Richard had died. I had never met Richard Walker but I travelled with him in my mind as each year he searched out new music and stories under the guise of an annual holiday. I was shocked by the effect that the announcement had on me. Part of my life just disappeared and yet I had never as much as been in the same room as him. Richard's departure marked a departure for me too. Though I have since dipped in and out of it, I have never regained the passion for folk music radio that he ignited.

I don't know what mid life crisis means for others but for me it was quite simple:
- I lost my way & I lost my self worth
- My children grew up and made their own decisions
- My wife and I lived separate lives
- My best friend and my wife's best friend both died

Mid Life Crisis

- We downsized our house.

Downsizing was a popular term in the early 1990's. Maggie Thatcher's Britain had given many of us a new found wealth. We had lived through the inflation years and seen the value of our properties grow. Downsizing, in theory, offered the opportunity to cash in that value and live a less financially demanding life. With my stint of unemployment, we had found it hard to pay a mortgage and the opportunity to rid ourselves of the responsibility was irresistibly seductive. What we failed to account for was that life is a compromise and there was a trade off. At a stroke, downsizing, denied our children the opportunity to visit the home they had grown up in. Their children, our grandchildren would also never see the home their parents had grown up in. Lifetimes experiences were translated into historical memory at the stroke of a pen. Living access to those memories was denied to past and future generations. Experiences became memories and were consigned to photograph albums and conversations. Sadly, the experience was so emotional that even to this day; I find it hard to talk about.

Mid Life Crisis

The week before we moved on to a "downsized" life of our choosing, the lorry arrived from The Donkey Sanctuary at Sidmouth to collect Jemma and Primrose, our two much loved donkeys. We had shared many experiences together, driving around the country lanes of Newport, Shropshire. We convinced ourselves that they were so interdependent that the loss of one would be terminal to the other. As such, we signed them away to the Sanctuary, at the same time, setting up a bank standing order to cover their costs in perpetuity. Seeing them loaded into the lorry left us in no doubt as to the enormity of our decision and if I could reverse that decision, I would have done so a thousand times. At the same time our best friend, Doug, died. His wife Helen, Jill's best friend, had been taken by cancer some years earlier and he was beginning to make a new life. He had a new lady in his life and they went on holiday together to Greece. He returned with Legionnaires Disease. I suffered a leg injury from Karate which resulted in an operation. On the day we moved, I went to Doug's funeral, on crutches with only one shoe. Jill supervised the house move (which became delayed by a week and resulted in living in a hotel). We seemed to suffer one bad experience after another. This was indeed the deepest pit of despair I have

ever known. If there was any bottoming to my life crisis this was it.

I seemed to lose all interest in anything. Every visit to Sidmouth was a painful reminder of what we had done. Primrose, one of two donkeys went into shock and ended up in intensive care. We were receiving thrice daily reports from the Sanctuary as to her wellbeing. Every weekend was a long journey to Devon and back. At the same time we were visiting Cheshire. Jill had missed Doug's funeral and goodbyes had to be said. Primrose eventually recovered and lived what we hope was a happy life until December 2006 when sadly she "went down" and died. Before then, following her recovery, every time we visited, one shout of "Primrose" would find her pushing her way though a group of 70 donkeys on a farm of 400, to get to us. Jemma, our other donkey never seemed to forgive us, especially after Primrose died. Oddly, in September 2007, when we visited her, she seemed at peace.

Mid Life Crisis

She was living in a group of 20 or so donkeys, all elderly, some blind, some like her arthritic. For the first time, whilst still sad, I felt the decision we had taken was right. She was on her own but had 24/7 care from the finest carers, in an environment in East Devon that is unparalleled in beauty, in a sanctuary that lives up in every way to its name. Our standing order still runs and we will always be forever indebted to the Donkey Sanctuary.

In this pit of despair, all interest in sport went. Life was a drudge and interest in anything pretty much went. I stopped playing in the band, stopped going to the folk club and pretty much stopped everything in life apart from work.

Losing the children had an enormous impact on us both. Our whole life had been lived, like our parents, with our children at its very centre. They had had good holidays, been to many places, done many things but all was in our control. Suddenly they were spreading their wings and we had no control at all. It is for them to tell there own stories if to do such a thing is ever their choosing, but for us, we seemed to lose our purpose. Clearly it was only the strength of us as a couple that

Mid Life Crisis

sustained our relationship and brought us through it.

Later in that same period of despair, we lost another friend. In all we lost 5 and each one chipped away at our resolve and our ability to cope with life or be normal folk. Chris was the partner to a friend of mine from Bradford. We learned that she had cancer. Much too-ing and fro-ing to Bradford ensued. Hours were spent on the telephone supporting her partner, Graham, whom I had worked with. They decided to get married. By this time she was wearing a wig and couldn't hide her condition. Her strength of character was an awesome thing to behold. She clung to hope and belief 24 hours a day. She would get better, she told herself.

The two of them had grand plans of retiring to Spain. They bought an apartment in Torrieveja. Due to medication she only got to see it once following diagnosis. Sadly she did not get better. She died in January 2005. I wrote a song as is my way:

The telephone rang and it was you
You turned our world from rose to blue
You said goodbye would be so soon
I couldn't take it in, I had no words for you

Another name, another friend, another diary date to end

Mid Life Crisis

Still there was time but not for fun
You were so strong and we were numb

You'll leave us memories of past times shared
Of hopes and dreams, emotions bared
When dealt the card you showed us how
That life's for living not then but now

You said ok that you could cope
And all along you gave us hope
Despair and loss is all that seems
But still you laugh and plan your dream

The telephone rings but it's not you

I don't know if I have ever come out of my mid life crisis. I would describe it as going into a crisis of life in my middle years. Am I out of it now aged nearly 60? No, if I am honest, I don't think I am. Life is better yes. The bottom that I bounced along for years is now not as deep, but the knocks of life keep coming. It must be the same for everyone. Each of us has his own tale and the horrors of life – war for example, rent terrible experiences on families and individuals. I can only tell my own story.

What I find difficult to comprehend is that apart from unemployment, and death, the sadnesses in my life have arisen largely from decisions over which I did exercise some control. I simply made the wrong decisions or made tough decisions at the required time.

Mid Life Crisis

There is an old saying "what you never had, you never miss". I have learned that what I did have, I do miss.

Reflecting now, I think I take the view that the mid life crisis is just the first conscious stage of growing old. We grow old from the time we are born. As a young hippy, I never expected to reach the age I have. Mid life crisis took away dreams, changed expectations and re contextualised my life in a way that I had no skills to deal with. Yes, like everyone, I had experienced family deaths but they were always of people older than me. As I got older I visualized future years using the current criteria the "isness" of that time in my life. I therefore envisaged my 40' and 50's in the context of friendships that death subsequently took away. Each experience seemed to have reduced my significance in relation to the world about me and the process goes on.

Bob Dylan wrote "I was engaged in a struggle I dare not fail".

For some reason I decided to be an entertainer and next day the 'phone rang!

Becoming A One Man Band

An entertainer eh!

Firstly, following all those years away from home. I decided that I was not going to work in pubs or clubs. This was going to be a nine to five job, five days a week, working from home.

Someone was listening that day. Jill and I were sat at in the kitchen talking about my becoming a full time entertainer and how I could fill in quiet times by helping in the

Becoming A One Man Band

family laundry business. The next day the telephone rang :

"Hello, is that Paul Woodhead"
"Yes"
"I got your name from the George Formby Society"
"Oh yes"
"I am warden of a sheltered housing scheme in Herefordshire and I have a couple living here who are celebrating their 60th wedding anniversary. Would you be able to come and sing some George Formby songs for them?"
"Why yes, I would be delighted"
"How much do you charge"
"Well what could you afford. Obviously I have to cover my travelling costs"
"Woulds £50 be alright, about an hour"
"Yes, that would be fine" .

My first booking was as simple and as coincidental as that. That first booking lead to others in Herefordshire, all of them unusual - The Rheumatic Society, Alzheimers, other sheltered groups, day care centres, retirement homes, harvest suppers, gardening clubs. I realised that I had stumbled into a niche, the niche was entertaining the 65 plus and even the 100 plus age group - mostly day time, mostly afternoons - an hour to an hour and a half.

Becoming A One Man Band

I decided that if this was to be what I did, then I would be the best entertainer of the elderly that there was. In retirement homes especially, I found out that most entertainers used the venues as fill ins for other more lucrative bookings eg gigs en route from one booking to another. As such, material was often innappropriate to the audience and was usually preformatted by way of a set list. I set about researching my target age group and realised that music from the 1930's to 1950's would serve 99% of expectations. Old music hall and World War 1 songs would add to my repertoire and be known to my audiences. I quickly built a song list to equal if not better any and began to use my guitar as well as my banjolele. I found that I could occasionally introduce songs that were not known to my audience as long as they were amusing and innoffensive. I called in at a local music shop once to see if they had any ukulele strings. They hadn't.

"But we do have an old broken ukulele you can have"
"There might be some strings on it".

I rebuilt that broken uke and introduced it to my act. I remembered the need for light and shade that I had learned with the Unicorn Folk

Becoming A One Man Band

Group. For my Formby songs, most of them being fast and furious, I used backing tracks. With the wooden uke, I found I could do singalong which people could join in with. With my guitar, I could pick or strum olde tyme standards as well as country songs and old time folk.

I tried to keep all my songs happy. Yes, there had to be the odd weepy and there was nothing wrong in that I learned. Old folk needed to cry occasionally and need to remember loved ones and special times in their lives. My music seemed to do that. But most of all, I wanted to make them happy, uplift them, take them to a happy place if only for an hour. I loved what I did and wherever I took them, we all went together.

I sat and taked to them, gained authentic knowledge of the music thay had grown up with. Not only did I learn these songs, I contextualised them – what film were they in, when was it made, who was in it, what was going on the world at that time? I became an authority on the songs I added to my repertoire.

I had some shocks along the way. A 94 year old man answered "Oh Lonesome Me" (1963) when asked his favouite song. Another

Becoming A One Man Band

gentleman in his 80's told me his favouurite was "Oh Carol" by Smokie. Another lady asked for "Mack The Knife" because no other visiting entertainer could or would sing it. I learned them all.

I found that because I showed an interest in their lives they gave of themselves. I was let into their world and learned even more. I talked to them during my concerts and discovered that it was easy to create a dialogue of memory exchange and reminiscence. I shied clear of songbooks and reminiscance scrapbooks, I wanted to engage them and hold them with the building blocks of my conversation and song and the cement of their memory and experience. My "gig" list was extensive. Christmas I could have run for three

Becoming A One Man Band

months. Disappointing people by not being able to fit them in was my fear.

I always felt it appropriate to dress to my audience. Thus, I would always wear a shirt and dicky bow, black trousers and a waistcoat. Weekend trips became a trawl of every High St charity shop looking for a new waistcoat. For my regular gigs, I ensured that I never repeated the same wasitcoat but rotated them. Audience comment would support my dress code.

I came up with the idea of building every month's concert around events of the month – births, deaths, films, history, calendar etc. This enabled me to introduce themes. Deaths were called "celebrations of life" rather than death. My themes took me into new areas of music that were unfamiliar to me. I was able to delve into Elvis and Jim Reeves as well as Daniel O'Donnel and Charlie Landsborough.

One day a lady died in her chair as I sang. On another day a gentleman who had been in care for 5 years and shown no interest in anything, just sat on his own, heard me play the spoons. A switch flicked on in his brain as he remembered he used to play them too. For the next year before he died, I entertained him bi

Becoming A One Man Band

monthly. He started organising the room in a concert setting and geting people into place. He raided the kitchen draw and assembled all his cutlery in front of him so that he could join in. He started getting out of his chair, because he wanted to. On the last day I entertained him, he danced with a care worker as I played "Anniversary Waltz" by Al Jolson.

In Birmingham I met a lady who claimed to be the wife of Frank Formby; in Kington, a man who claimed that George's younger sister was his first girlfriend. In Birmingham I entertained an ex circuit judge and two retired opera singers, in Bilston, a headmaster, a police inspector and a lady of the night, in South Birmingham a lady who said Raymond Froggatt's mum was her best friend and that she remembered Froggie and Ozzie Osbourne as "snotty nosed kids"; white people, Asians, Africans, young men with early Alzheimers, old women with a teenagers sex drive, young people who found themselves in care with elderly people because there was nowhere else for them to go (they wanted rock music), Downs Syndrome, learning difficulties and so on.

Once I had a request from a gentleman for "I'll Take You Home Kathleen". His wife who was visiting him elbowed him and they then had a

Becoming A One Man Band

row. She came to me later and explained that they had only been married two years when he had an affair. The lady in question was named Kathleen.

I entertained the Irish who all want "Danny Boy", Germans (who like "Happy Wanderer", Norwegians (who just go "Yah, Yah" whatever you sing) and Russians who for some reason love George Formby. In Normandy, the French allowed me to indulge my memory of their language. I remembered that one verse was about a French "lady of the night" and had to "anglicise" my French so as not to cause offence. In Tenerife, the Spanish just thought I was an eccentric Englishman.

One day after a concert south of Birmingham. I called in a local music store and saw a strange intrument called a Suzuki Q. I had bought a Yamaha PSR 2000 keyboard for home use as I refused to use bought in backing tracks and for certain songs eg George Formby, accompanying music was essential. My audiences would hear my efforts only. I had no wish to build any success on the strength of what I could afford by way of studio produced backing music. To this day it depresses me deeply to hear people praising the efforts of an artist, oblivious to the fact that most of what they hear he/she has bought ie the effort of

Becoming A One Man Band

someone else. Notwithstanding that, I had learned in my pursuit of light and shade that my audiences liked to hear strings and brass, even when I was playing banjolele so I had to have a backing. Other songs, such as country music, often benefitted from having a "genre" backing suited to the song eg steel guitar. Also sometimes, with my early Portastudio, I could add my own harmonies so that they could hear me sing with myself.

The Suzuki Q stood in a window. It was burgundy in color, plastic and shaped like nothing I had ever seen. I could see that it had on board rhythms and something called a strumplate. I went in the shop and asked what it was. The owner was less than knowledgable about it but suggested he got one down from the shelf and let me feel my way around it. I learned that it was a second generation Omnichord, though I had no knowledge of what a first generation instrument was. In

Becoming A One Man Band

simple terms it had 12 onboard rhythms with various controls over each rhythm ie certain intrumentation could be knocked out. Additionally it had a 4 octave strumplate which could be set to any one of 99 midi sounds. It could be strummed like a guitar or touched to sound like a harp or a vibe or one of many other sounds. It was described as a "Digital Guitar" but I thought it more like a digital autoharp with automatic accompaniement. It could also be bought with an add on rhythm cartridge which increased its rhythm capabilities or with song cartridges that autoplayed a range of songs. The song cartridges appealed not at all as I thought that was the ultimate in cheating an audience.

I came out of the shop with a Q and an add on rhythm cartridge (giving me a total of 42 rhythms).

I carefully put together a range of songs using every rhythm at my disposal. Some were unusable for me eg dance music and techno but most were ok. The left hand played the rhythm chord and the right the strumplate. The left hand was laid out in button format like a button accordian. I found that I could talk to my audiences and carry on playing, just like my acoustic guitar. There were no pre formatted boundaries as in pre recorded

Becoming A One Man Band

backing music. Leaving out the rhythms, I discovered the facility to "ape" a church organ for hymns and create my version of the wail of a pipe for Irish and Scottish song.

Later I was to incorporate the Q into One Man Band and learned how to play it with a drum stick attached to my banjolele.

I learned that making mistakes was ok. This was live music. In fact not only was it ok, it often added comedy value (remember Les Dawson). I began to look for opportunities to get things wrong always trying to ensure that the audience never knew whether it was deliberate or not. That way, when I genuinly did get it wrong, everyone just thought it was part of the act.

In my pursuit for light and shade, I went back to my own dad's music. I bought a new harmonica. I had played around with one in the Unicorn Folk Group but never really pursued it. I set about playing melody and bought a C,D, G and A version, the four keys I thought I would use most. I took some of my old "crooning" type songs from the 1930's and replaced a string instrument with the harmonica. So, using just my backing or the Q and the harmonica I could really sing a song without worrying what fingers to put where

Becoming A One Man Band

on the fretboard of whatever I was playing. When I knew what I was doing, I added back the guitar and put the harmonica in a mouth truss, Bob Dylan style. I could sense my own development.

There was a chap in the George Formby Society called George Chisholm. He would sit on stage at Blackpool during convention weekends and provide a "bones" contribution to the backing band. The bones are two pieces of wood shaped like a rib bone. My audiences call them the "clappers". I decided to learn the bones and once whilst up in Bradford visiting our friends, we went to Saltaire. There in a shop was a set of Irish bones complete with instructions. I set about learning them and with help from a chap called Walter Kirkland, again a George Formby Society member, I quickly mastered the basics. Getting up on stage with Walter was a months practice in three minutes. He has to be the best bones player I have ever known . George Chisholm left us a few years ago now. Probably playing his bones in the sky.

One Christmas I provided the entertainment for the Telford Sequence Dancing Club.

A lady came to me at the end of the evening :

Becoming A One Man Band

"I really enjoyed listening to the bones, my husband used to play them"
"Thank you very much. He doesn't play them now?"
"No, he died a few years ago. I have his bones in a box in the bedroom"
(Had to thnk about that)
"Would you like them"
"That's very kind"
"I'll go and fetch them whilst you clear away"

Whilst I was packing up my stuff, she went home. She returned with a pair of genuine bone "bones" , each wrapped in tissue paper. They were pure cream like ivory. She proceeded to tell me how on D Day, petrified by what lay ahead, her husband had gone to the mess canteen before embarkation and acquired a pair of sheep or cow ribs. The crossing to France was made easier for him by being mentally immersed in the conversion of these animal ribs to musical bones. They survived his war years and he played them until his death. Fifty odd years after he crafted them, I held them in my hand - a piece of history. But how could I repay? I decided, now that I had two sets, I must become ambidextrous ie a two handed player, so I did. Every year, I now play her bones back to her. I have only ever seen one other person play two

Becoming A One Man Band

handed so I think that is a fitting tribute to her husband.

I was once booked to entertain at one of these party political events in Redditch. The sort where the hopeful or sitting MP tells everyone that he/she has a policy just for them – old, young and in the cradle. A cross section of the population is there, from the Cubs to the pensioners. I met a very elderly bones player. I don't know what he had been in life but he was now elderly, frail and not as mentally fit as he probably once was. He had a bag of musical bits and pieces and nearly fell off his chair when I got my bones out. He got his out too. The audience loved it. He was the centre of attention, never mind the dignatories. He had the afternoon of his life. Sadly, he wanted me to take him home. He obviously thought the rest of his life could be lived every minute like the past hour. Oh were that possible!! I have met him several times since, always with his bones.

Whilst in Dublin, I bought a set of Siamese spoons ie musical spoons joined at the handle, more befitting the title "clappers". I felt my way around them experimenting with various positions. Then via GOOGLE, I found some instructions on playing spoons on the internet. It helped me procure an appropriately shaped

Becoming A One Man Band

pair from a boot sale and I began my "spoons" career! No other instrument captivates my audience like the spoons. I learned to play them sat down or stood up. I learned the little intricacies of technique. Most of all, I incorporated the showmanship necessary to make them a show all on their own. I produced some fitting music on my keyboard, tunes I knew my audiences would know and away we went. During one afternoon concert, I even taught the basics to a young man who then joined in with me, much to the delight of my audience.

I met another spoons player in Tenerife, a little Irishman, much like a leprechaun. He was playing spoons in a restaurant and I crept up behind him (having raided the restaurant cutlery draw). We played spoons for hours with my friend Ged Roberts providing the main attraction on keyboard and vocals. The audience loved it. There aren't many nights in life when you are entertained by a spoons player. And two? Well beyond one's wildest dreams!!

The Unicorn Folk Group was an Irish band. One of our members, Ted Drury, played mandolin, brilliantly. I have loved the mandolin ever since. I decided to add one to my growing "orchestra". I discovered one I

Becoming A One Man Band

was comfortable playing in a music shop in Newtown in Wales. I will never be as good as Ted but I am good enough and I can always throw the odd simple bluegrass tune or instrumental fill into any of my songs. Also, the mandolin is great for some country music and even my Morecambe and Wise songs! "Donald Where's Yoor Troosers" goes down well too!

One show I did was as a part of a Concert Party, led by a chap called John KirkPatrick of folk fame. It was held at Bishops Castle Community College. We were doing a musical evening called "Tunes from the Trenches". This was all songs from WW1 and WW2 with spoken introduction. My contribution was a George Formby rendition called "I Did What I Did With My Gas Mask". It went down very well but the highlight for me was that we formed a comb and paper orchestra. How could I recreate that sound whilst keeping my hands free to do other things? The answer lay in a KAZOO. Attached to my mouth truss, next to my harmonica it is a perfect facsimile.

My daily pursuit is light and shade. The uniqueness I seek is to take my audience on a rollercoaster of musical sound – loud, quiet, orchestral backing and acoustic. I dip into every type of music except opera. I go from

Becoming A One Man Band

Waltz to Charleston, from Quickstep to Jive. Musically, I no longer draw heavily from George Formby. I stick to George's songs that I know my audience will know adding in others that have calendar or historical significance. For example I celebrate the building of Britain's first public laundry house in Salford by singing George's "Chinese Laundry Blues". I sing songs that are country, folk, jazz, pop, religous, showtime, wartime indeed anything that I enjoy doing that I know my audience will remember or appreciate. I also write a lot of my own and slip the odd one in when appropriate.

I find that elderly people like a strong beat. I decided to introduce some marching music but felt that I would have to march to complete the delivery. I was watching the morris men in Ironbridge one day and decided to make what I call my "stomper stick". New Years Day and I was in the garage dismembering the sweeping brush and a "Bex Bissell" floor cleaner. I took the sweeping brush stale, added the Bex Bissel handle, put a door stop on the bottom (to protect wooden floors), added some loose bottle tops on ribbons and screws, a couple of bells from goodness knows where and finished off with some Christmas decorations. I then took a spare KAZOO and fashioned some gas tubing into a circle with an

Becoming A One Man Band

ASDA food funnel at the end. It looked like a trumpet! I now had a marching stick and a trumpet. I put together some marching songs and yet another dimension was added to my repertoire.

A friend of mine, a professional guitarist, had a stroke and because he was unable to play, sold off his equipment. One item was an AER Domino Acoustic Cube amplifier with four channels and built in effects. I bought it and now had seperate lines into the amp for each of my stringed instruments- no more

Becoming A One Man Band

unplugging. I then decided that if I could set everything up in advance of a concert, the day would be easier and I would save time. Elderly people can quickly become impatiemt. I opted for a sack truck. The Domino sits on the sack truck but can be lifted off to load in the car. All the leads for every instrument were attached to the sack truck and colour co ordinated. I needed something for my Q. I decided to mount part of a conductor stand on the handle of the sack truck. The stand held the Q, and provided fixing points for a guitar hanger and a ukulele hanger (I no longer needed to carry guitar stands). The holes in the stand were drilled out to accept my spoons, kazoo and other bits and pieces. At this point, I could no longer see the amp which impeded volume control (critical if entertaining older people because of hearing aids). I decided to buy a small cheap mixer desk and affix it to the front of my sack truck facing me. I found an old bodrhan (irish drum) and mounted it on the front (so none of the wires and the mixer were visible). I then surrounded the drum with multicoloured Christmas lights. I then got a string puppet (Fred), mounted him on the drum and via pulleys and string attached his controls to my feet.

I could make Fred dance!

Becoming A One Man Band

I had my first One Man Band.

Over the years, my sack truck model has undergone countless modifications. I must now be at version 10 or more. The fundamental concept remains the same. I wheel it in, plug it in, switch on my mp3 player and my audience immediately has music. I can then take as long as I choose to set up. I can actually be ready to go in 10 to 15 minutes because everything is pre set.

Some things that I have bought / acquired over the years have taken my performance to a new level. One of these is a radio head mic. I can wander about and personalise what I do "on the fly". Apart from my memory jogger of diary events that month eg births and deaths, no concert is planned. Part of my success at what I do is the sponteneity. No set list restricts a performance. I actually have no idea what I am going to do until I get there. When setting up, I am listening for people's names, what they had for lunch; anything to give me a clue of where to start. A field of sheep seen through the window might suggest starting with "Will You Love Me When I'm Mutton As You Love Me Now I'm Lamb" by Gracie Fields. A planned outing being chattered about might trigger "Summer Holiday" by

Becoming A One Man Band

Cliff Richard. Anyone called "Daisy" or "Charmaine" has no chance!!

On the minus side, I bought a looping machine. In my pursuit for live music I thought a looper would enable me to create songs "looping" in all the various things I do; and it does. I use it often but never now for my elderly audiences. It goes over their heads and does not add value.

My sack truck One Man Band is now known as my digital system. It incorporates the Suzuki Q and is of course amplified. I use it daily for my "over 60's" work. I use it on stage and at anywhere that people want to dance. With full orchestration from the Q, I can go anywhere musically, limited only by my own ability and sense of adventure.

As well as my elderly audience, I began to get bookings for private functions, garden parties clubs and even hospitals and hospices. One such booking was at a "Festival of Eccentric Music". At the end of my stage set a man came up to me and said : "If you had a big drum, you'd be a One Man Band". Obviously he didn't see me as a OMB even though that is what I was introduced as. In that the nature of one man banding for me

Becoming A One Man Band

is driven by a desire to improve and meet any expectation. I knew I needed an acoustic version.

I experimented with various alternatives but eventually settled on a suitcase bass drum with a washboard mounted on the top. The washboard is attached to the drum beater and is played by bottle tops scraping the washboard. Next to this, I have a percussion stand on which I have cowbells, wood blocks, cymbals etc which I play with a stick attached to my right arm. I also house a teapot and a jug. My right foot plays the suitcase bass. My left foot plays tambourine. Instead of the uke, banjolelele or Martin Backpacker guitar, I dug out my 12 string from the folk club days.

People's expectations vary but in Britain, we associate "One Man Band" with a drum on the back and indeed I realised that there was a market for just such a thing. Using all my experience gained to date I developed such a system. I tried and failed several times. I bought drums off eBay only to resell them because they were not what I wanted. In the end I got there but the process goes on. It seems that each winter I think of improvements that I can incorporate. These usually result in a complete rebuild!

Becoming A One Man Band

Equally, my mouth truss undergoes continuous development. It curretly comprises – harmonica, kazoo, siren, whistle, duck call and oil filler pipe!

Simultaneously, I built a website www.woodysonemanband.co.uk and began to be found by bookers and agents wanting one man band entertainment. Rates of pay were much, much higher. I found a market with street carnivals and festivals. One thing that has surprised me with this market is that so little of it is local. I pick up my local newspaper every week and see local fayres and street events yet I rarely get a booking. My work tends to come from far afield and seems to be driven by GOOGLE. To be fair, I keep so busy that I make little effort to find new work so I just let it go by.

I have learned over the years never to prejudge a gig. Always expect the unexpected. One booking took me up north of Wigan to a large outdoor carnival and fair. I was booked as a "troubador" one man band ie a walkabout entertainer. I took no amplification, no Q, no keyboard, just my acoustic rigs. It was a glorious summers day when we set up the motorhome in the local town park. I strapped my bass drum on my back, morris dancers bells on my legs, and guitar in hand set off

Becoming A One Man Band

through the crowds. The fair had a central arena for all the usual dog shows etc. Around the arena were concessions from candy floss to magic glass cleaning products, from hamburgers to black peas. I wandered about engaging folk in ones and twos, a photo here and there (people like photos especially with their children), the odd request for a tune or song. I would creep up on folk and blow my siren whistle and generally join in with the good time they appeared to be having. On one occasion I got told off because the whippets were lining up for a race and the siren and drum frightened them. I learned that whippet racing is serious stuff in Lancashire, in fact it turned out to be that main event of the day – besides whippet racing, I am sure there was a whippet best of breed show, most obedient whippet, oldest whippet, youngest whippet, biggest whippet, smallest whippet! Of course these were only the adult competitions. Every one was duplicated for children! Then there was the teenager and whippet shows!!

"Woody, Woody" came the cry.
"One of the bands has let us down. Can you do a spot on stage?"

A spot on stage turned out to be an hour and all I had was my suitcase bass, drum on back

Becoming A One Man Band

and guitar. No amplification, just the MC's mic and a crowd in their thousands.

Lesson – be prepared for the unexpected!

One of my favourite outdoor gigs has to be the local Teddy Bear festival in Ironbridge, Shropshire. Located in the beautiful Dale Park, Ironbridge, on the banks of the River Severn, I was able to park right next to where I was due to play. I was booked to play for the day and for the previous two years as well as subsequently, due to other bookings, I have not been free to accept the gig. In 2006, I was able to accept the booking which was simply to entertain the crowds. I was told that many had travelled from overseas and that the busiest part of the day would be lunchtime when because of lunch being included in their

Becoming A One Man Band

ticket price, a large queue would form outside the hospitality tent. "Could I keep them occupied?"

A canopy tent had been set up for me and I organised myself beneath it. I had everything with me – sacktruck OMB, suitcase bass and walkabout bass drum on the back. I had all my intruments from keyboard to ukulele and I had my large PA system. For the first couple of hours I sang and played middle of the road stuff in keeping with the slow pace and beauty of the day. Teddy Bears were to be seen everywhere. The festival was funded and promoted by "Merrythought Ltd", a local manufacturer of hand crafted Teddies. They had a worldwide collectors club hence the international audience. In the auction tent were beautiful examples of collectors Teddies which were to be auctioned later in the day by a TV celebrity. Visitors could also tour the factory and meet the skilled workforce, many of whom had done particular "teddy" jobs for years eg making eyes or noses. All of this added to the day and authenticated the experience for visitors.

Becoming A One Man Band

I was given three objectives :
1. Generally entertain the passers by from my stationary position.
2. Towards the end of the day to "troubador" around the factory as visitors were educated in the various functions of teddy making.
3. Most importantly keep the dinner queue engaged for 30 minutes or so as they waited to be served.

Becoming A One Man Band

As the morning wore on, whilst there were clearly several hundred people in attendace, they were scattered across the site so at no time was I aware of numbers. At around 12.30pm I was tipped that buffet lunch was to be served. As though from nowhere, hundreds of people started queueing outside the hospitality tent. I donned my bass drum and wandered over to the front of the queue only to learn that the hospitality tent wasn't quite ready. In fact it took a further 30 minutes. I began entertaining small clusters of people who slowly got more and more agitated and more and more angry as time went on. My 30 minute troubador set lasted 2 hours and in the summer sun I was exhausted! I am glad to say that we got through it and though a few tempers were frayed everyone was ok in the end.

Troubadoring the teddy bear factory was less successful. One thing you learn as a One Man Band is that although still essentially a "short vehicle", you are a lot longer than everyone else!

I gave up in the end on health and safety grounds!

Trade Fairs, Festivals and Street Entertaining

For several years I have entertained at the "Country Music Trade Fair" in Bristol. It is an opportunity to entertain an audience of club managers, agents and festival organisers. As an entertainer, one of my characteristics is that I dip into all sorts of music. Like for every positive there is also a negative, in my case my "dipping" is also one of my problems. As a performing One Man Band, I don't really belong anywhere other than in front of a street audience!

Now in front of a George Formby Appreciation Society audience I am known as a "country" singer. I guess I take the view that there are other better players than me so I just do my own thing. They interpret my style as "country". Equally, in front of a country music loving audience I am often thought of as a George Formby singer. It is very confusing.

My first performance at the Bristol Country Music Trade Fair in 2005 (the 13th but I had missed the first 12), probably sums it up. In those days there was a national country music newspaper and a chap called Bob Dixon whom I now know to be the superb steel

Trade Fairs, Festivals and Street Entertaining

guitar player in a top UK country band called Kalibre, had been asked to report on the artists who performed. I was booked to play all three days and the first night, Saturday, was singer songwriter night so all the songs I sang were from my own pen. Bob wrote : " *Nothing had prepared me for the next performer, Paul Woodhead from Shropshire, known as Woodys One Man Band. This slightly eccentric character wheeled his instruments and effects, along with his miniature mixing desk, all attached to a sack truck with gaffa tape, pipe lagging and cable ties onto stage, to the incredulous expression of the now growing audience. He launched into a set of songs that can best be described as a cross between George Formby, Don Partridge and old time music hall sing along. I can think of nothing further removed from country music than this and anyone who can write a song with the title "I Stole A Sausage While My Darlin' Wasn't Looking" gets my vote for sheer impudence. I loved his slightly camp delivery and his ad-libs and the audience reaction to his show said it all. They loved him and as an entertainer, he is first class. He was rather put out that he did not have time to play his frying pan but as they say that's wok'n roll."*

On the Sunday I gave my second performance: *"The second act to grace stage two*

Trade Fairs, Festivals and Street Entertaining

was Woodys One Man Band again and he gave another performance that was sheer entertainment. His material was a little more "country" than the Saturday show and he bumbled his way through the set with an almost Tommy Cooper like ineptitude that kept the audience laughing throughout."

On Monday, I gave my third performance : *"Woodys One Man Band was next up and again floored the audience with a mixture of songs, both standards and originals, that no matter how hard you tried could never be taken seriously. Of course, it's not meant to be serious stuff and I must give credit to Woody for keeping us amused both on and off stage. Woody is to country music what Arthur Mullard was to ballet, but as a cabaret act, first class".*

Trade Fairs, Festivals and Street Entertaining

Now I am sure there are some who are wondering "Who was Arthur Mullard?" Well, the first thing that occurs to me as I write is that anyone who quotes Arther Mullard as a reference point must have a long memory or be quite old themselves.

I quote from Wikepedia :

"From a humble background, he (Arthur Mullard) was born in Islington, and started work at 14 as a butcher's assistant, and went on to join the Army at 18. It was during his time in the army that he began boxing, and duly became the champion boxer of his regiment. When

Trade Fairs, Festivals and Street Entertaining

he eventually left the Army he did actually have a short stint at boxing professionally.

Following the end of the Second World War in 1945 the burly ex-boxer sought out work as a stuntman at the Pinewood and Ealing film studios, from which he drifted into uncredited bit-parts in classic British films such as Oliver Twist, The Ladykillers, The Belles of St. Trinians, Chitty Chitty Bang Bang and The Lavender Hill Mob.

Mullard's distinctive "ugly mug" appearance and particular variety of cockney accent lent itself to a certain character and pretty soon he graduated to more visible roles in comedy films and on television. It was on television where Arthur Mullard truly made a name for himself, firstly as a straight man for the likes of Tony Hancock, Frankie Howerd and Benny Hill, and he starred in The Arthur Askey Show. It was the London Weekend Television series Romany Jones, first aired in 1973, which give Mullard his highest profile, playing the part of Wally Briggs, a crafty caravan-dwelling character.

So popular was Mullard's character in Romany Jones that a spin-off series - Yus, My Dear - was created in 1976, where Wally and his wife Lily (Queenie Watts) had moved out of their caravan into a council house. The series introduced a new character, Wally's brother Benny, the first acting role for future EastEnders and Snatch star Mike Reid. Yus, My Dear was a smash hit and Arthur (or "Arfur" as he was widely known) was

Trade Fairs, Festivals and Street Entertaining

regularly seen as a guest star in other programmes and even in television commercials.

Such was Mullard-mania in the late seventies that the man even graced the pop charts in 1978 with his own rendition of "You're The One That I Want" (originally from the movie Grease) in a duet with Hylda Baker (who was also in her sixties). It might have been an even bigger hit, but a live appearance by the two veteran comic performers on the BBC TV show Top Of The Pops was such a disaster (Mullard and Baker fluffed the lyrics and seemed utterly confused as to what was happening) that record sales plummeted spectacularly after the broadcast.

The hit single was to be the last great success of Mullard's life, and following an uncredited narration on the Glenn Close- led live action 101 Dalmatians (which screened in 1996), he died in his sleep on 11 December 1995.

Mullard continued to live in a council maisonnette in Islington after his film and television success and to spend much of his leisure time in the local pubs. In a newspaper interview after his death, Arthur Mullard's daughter, Barbara, claimed that he had sexually abused her for years and had driven her mother to commit suicide. "His friends,' she said, 'weren't surprised".

Bit of a back handed compliment that one!

Trade Fairs, Festivals and Street Entertaining

Similarites – well yes, I do bumble, I do get confused , I do fluff the lyrics and forget them (that might explain lack of repeat bookings?).

Differences – well I don't think I look like an ex boxer, I drink very little, I never sexually abused my daughter (not least of which because I have two sons). Oh yes – I never met Hilda Baker!

I love the Trade Fair. As a performer, it is a rare opportunity to see other acts. I find as an entertainer, that generally I don't really want to go out anywhere or see anybody so the Trade Fair is an opportunity to redress that. I have done three now. I still haven't quite cracked the "country" feel except in my head. I have a song that I wrote back in 2005 :

Well I know I'm not pure country, maybe I can't sing like Garth

But my head is full of Bob Dixon's guitar

Yes, I've got a country heart.

You may see me here as a jester just playing around for my part

But when I sing to myself, I hear Jimmie and Hank

'Cos for me they were the start.

Trade Fairs, Festivals and Street Entertaining

Well I know I'm not pure country, bluegrass beyond my art

But I do the best, with the junk that I find

Suitcase, teapot, guitar.

Well I know I'm not pure country but I have a country heart.

I guess that my song sums me up quite well. I came to find country music as a result of being in the Unicorn Folk Band. Most of the songs we sang were Irish though a few were English and Scottish and some American. I remember that we had songs like **"This Land Is Your Land"** by Woodie Guthrie. I could identify with that because of my John Steinbeck studies with *"Grapes of Wrath"*. I was in the local library one day and I came across a CD by a old time singer called **Jimmie Rogers**. I had never heard of him but his picture on the CD cover reminded me of a bloke that sang in our folk club. I thought it might be a hoot to take it and kid the audience that our local singer had a CD out. The resemblance was convincingly uncanny. I took the CD home and decided to have listen to it. Seems strange

Trade Fairs, Festivals and Street Entertaining

now to think that back then there were no CD players in cars. Cassettes were still the thing as CD's were still a home play only medium.

Back at home, **Jimmie Rodgers** sang our from my player. He sang from a time in the early 1920's to 1930's period, **Woody Guthrie** times, **"Grapes of Wrath"** times. I read the cover insert which was unusually comprehensive, and learned that Jimmie was born in 1897 in Mississippee, the third son of an Ohio railway worker. He had an affinity for travel and was entertaining by the age of 13, twice having disappeared with travelling music shows. Eventually he went to work on the railway and they became his inspirational source for writing songs. In 1924, at the age of 27, he contracted tubercolosis (TB) and his railway life was curtailed. In 1927, Jimmie was recorded by a mobile recording studio, The Talking Machine Company. He had modest success but then with his "Blue Yodel" and "T For Texas" went on to sell half a million copies. After that he sold out theatres across America. By 1933, he had succumbed to TB and was dead. Jimmie Rodgers is

Trade Fairs, Festivals and Street Entertaining

acknowledged as the father of Country music. His website reads :

"His is the music of America. He sang the songs of the people he loved, of a young nation growing strong. His was an America of glistening rails, thundering boxcars, and rain-swept night, of lonesome prairies, great mountains and a high blue sky. He sang of the bayous and the cornfields, the wheated plains, of the little towns, the cities, and of the winding rivers of America."

I had found old time country music and though my love of the music grew very selectively and excludes most things past the 1950's, my love of Jimmie Rodgers continues to this day. I think for me, it is also the love of acoustic music and recordings which lack technology. Though it is difficult today to compare even the most basic home recording studio with anything Jimmie Rodgers would have recorded on, nonetheless, part of my One Man Band endeavour is to try and be true to the sound I can create live and not overdub or mess about after the event. Most OMB recordings I do in one take. Not necessarily the first, but still one.

Trade Fairs, Festivals and Street Entertaining

The country music scene is a very confusing one here in the UK. We have some superb true country acts such as Bob Dixon's, Kalibre, a band comprising three superb live musicians. Central to the UK scene is Raymond Froggatt and his band, comprising H Cain and various lineups. Probably not a pure country sound, Froggie was adopted by the country music scene many years ago and has introduced thousands of people over the years to their local country music club, where they have grown into the UK country sound. These people are superb live performers and together with a select group of like minded performers lead the UK scene. Unfortunately, also in their midst, are the "karaoke" boys. Buy a backing tape for a fiver from a recording house and then sing along, usually with a guitar hung around the neck. I have no issue with singers who have backing music, they make no pretence that the sound is coming from a mini disk player or the like. They are selling their voice. I do however take issue with others who pretend that they are in some way contributing to the sound the audience is hearing when in fact their instrument is turned all the way down and the

Trade Fairs, Festivals and Street Entertaining

whole "playing" performance is little more than a mime act. Sadly, there are a number of them and some of them have reached great success off the back of other people's musical skills.

Audiences seem to make no distinction between authenticity and mime and sadly, as a solo performer, if one strives for success, the backing track route seems the easiest option. At the end of the day, audiences are there to be entertained. They have paid good money and taken the trouble to leave their warm home to see you the entertainer. The stage is not the venue for politicising the music scene and for year's bands and combos have struggled to find venues that can pay them a living wage for plying their craft. The result of this is backing tracks and karaoke singers, a product of recent times. I regret to say that even I have to do it, but my One Man Band is my acoustic release. My philosophy is the slogan of the Musicians Union *"keep music live"*. How else can you possibly know the true quality of what you are hearing?

One faction of the country music scene that appears to have resisted the temptation is

Trade Fairs, Festivals and Street Entertaining

bluegrass. Usually made up of fine acoustic musicians, bluegrass enjoys a huge following here in the UK.

Oddly, the music genre that I came from, folk, is the opposite way around. Entertainment is probably secondary to musicianship (says he, finger in ear)!

One great opportunity for an act like mine is in the field of charity fund raising. From back in my folk days to date, I have played for charity fundraising events. For me these events are usually outside and allow me to hone my "troubadour" style One Man Band. I entertain in the street, outside pubs and even in ASDA! The ASDA show was on behalf of a local hospice and a team of drummers entertained the shoppers inside, whilst I entertained and collected money in the entrance to the store.

Carnivals, festivals and street fayres are all natural venues for an act like mine.

Trade Fairs, Festivals and Street Entertaining

Adlington Carnival, Near Wigan, Lancashire.

Trade Fairs, Festivals and Street Entertaining

JABBERWOCKY – "What sort of a name is that?" I thought when I received an eMail in June 2007 from an events management company.

Jabberwocky, is of course, is a poem from Lewis Carroll's Alice in Wonderland.

Jabberwocky steers a fine literary course between being understood and being nonsense.

Alice said *"It seems very pretty," when she had finished it, "but it's rather hard to understand!" (You see she didn't like to confess even to herself, that she couldn't make it out at all.)*

"Somehow it seems to fill my head with ideas--only I don't exactly know what they are! "

A Disney TV company were filming a new preschool puppet film called Bunnytown and I received an email from Jabberwocky Events asking me if I would be interested in performing as a one man band. Filming was scheduled for June 24th, 2007 at Elstree Studios in Borehamwood.

It came and went too quickly. Following a dreadful journey on Saturday (because of M1

Trade Fairs, Festivals and Street Entertaining

closure), we arrived at Elstree Film & Television Studios at around 11.30pm. Instead of reading the instructions properly, I had gone to the village of Elstree instead of going to Borehamwood and as such driven around the area for an hour looking in the wrong place. Security had already reserved a parking spot for the motorhome in a secluded place (next to the main road) but at least secure & safe. We had travelled the night before filming as I had to be up at 6am next morning for makeup & costume at the ungodly hour of 7.30am. I duly reported to security who directed me to Room 41 of the John Maxwell Building. John Maxwell took over Elstree Studios quite early in its life and signed up a young Alfred Hitchcock. Hitchcock filmed what is regarded as Britain's firs "talkie" called "Blackmail". Back in the 1930's Elstree was launching the careers of great talents such as Charles Laughton, Laurence Olivier, Googie Withers and Stewart Grainger. I remember all of these stars especially Googie Withers. She had appeared with George Formby's in the 1939 film "Trouble Brewing".

Makeup included the mirror on the wall with light bulbs around & everyone was very jolly considering the time in the morning. I was brushed with lots of foundation but didn't

Trade Fairs, Festivals and Street Entertaining

think I looked any better after it. Oddly enough, when it was over & I removed my shirt, the neckline was stained brown with makeup. The experience doesn't tempt me to cross dress and male cosmetics hold no more appeal than they did before. Transvestism is not for me!!

From makeup it was off to costume where a very upbeat chap said with delight that I was already dressed perfectly. I had been asked to dress as I would normally busk so I had elected to wear top hat and tails with denim jeans, One Man Band boots (have to have attachment for operating OMB) and a white shirt. I thank Julie from Triplestop films (Channel 4, The Busker Symphony) for much of that look. She had an eye for a detail which I remembered well from 2006.

Knowing this film was for America & having been asked when they booked me to remove my Union Jack & St Georges flag, I simply replaced my very English deerstalker with a more universally recognised top hat. I have a puppet crow which was also attached to my coat.

Trade Fairs, Festivals and Street Entertaining

Everyone was on the film set (Stage 5) by 8am. I was one of two extras brought in, both of us for specific reasons. The other chap was a gymnast & I was booked as a walkabout One Man Band. Contractual restrictions prevent me from describing the set, the actors or the subject matter but I can say that the film was called Bunnytown and anyone GOOGLING that will learn that it is an animated puppet film for TV.

At 8am precisely, just as though a switch had flicked, filming began. Everyone knew what to do (except us two extras). Filming took place until 1pm and my slot ran from 11am for about 40 minutes. It was the last day of filming though I don't know how long they had been going. The whole thing resulted in a contribution measured in seconds rather than minutes though as a recognisable extra, credits were given to Woody's One Man Band. Typically the contract signed away intellectual property or any other future claim and gave sole ownership, quite rightly, in this case, to the Disney production company.

Trade Fairs, Festivals and Street Entertaining

The attention to detail was incredible and the experience was unique. As with my previous media experience with Triplestop in 2006, I was left mouth open by the skill, professionalism, dedication and single mindedness of what was in this case an entirely self employed, jobbing, contract crew.

Logistically, the whole thing was planned to minutest detail requiring on the fly management at macro and micro level. As the studio's are forward booked for weeks, months and years ahead, it is impossible to revisit something forgotten hence the relentless filming from every angle in various lightings etc etc.

It was fascinating to see a crew of about 30, each responsible for their own specific things. Credits at the end of a film list people with odd titles and there they all were from "Runners" to Boom Holders.

The Elstree site is fascinating and of course is home to many famous and loved films and TV programmes. Every corridor is lined with photographs and there is a memorial wall

Trade Fairs, Festivals and Street Entertaining

outside in recognition of well known English comedy genius - Carry On films, On The Buses, Bless This House etc. Famous visitors to the studio include Charlie Chaplin and Stan Laurel. Other famous comedy actors to grace Elstree "boards" include Terry Thomas, Charlie Drake & Tony Hancock.

Other famous names who filmed at Elstree include Ronald Reagan, Marlene Dietrich, Richard Harris, Cliff Richard, Sean Connery, Ingrid Bergman.

Sadly Elstree is also known for the "Big Brother" series and on Sunday the queues to get into the house area were testament to its success (though I must confess to not being a fan). The studio had allowed us to park our motorhome in the car park, in fact they had reserved us a space. On the morning following filming, I was awoken by the sound of human voices. I looked out of the window to see the long "Big Brother", literally hundreds of people.

Thankfully the studio has many greater claims to fame - Hitchcock films, three Star Wars films, the Indiana Jones trilogy to name but a

Trade Fairs, Festivals and Street Entertaining

few. For contractual reasons I cannot discuss the "gig" further other than it was a new Disney production scheduled for the US market and subsequent worldwide TV distribution. I was told that BBC and SKY had already committed to buy.

Being an entertainer of the type I am takes me to strange and unexpected audiences. I have done two years with SAGA Holidays on their historical tours. Based at Birmingham University, I have worked with brass bands, silver bands and a medieval quartet. Other interesting audiences have included the Pentecostal Church and the Salvation Army. The Army is a great audience as the members are well used to feeling free to express themselves. If the music takes them they will get up and dance and will always join in the fun of the moment. I have treated them to my one man band rigs in all it's formats though marching around "troubadour style" seems to bring out the best in them!

Once on holiday I was able to join a friend in the Cyprus Ukulele Band. We performed on stage in a huge theatre with a full orchestra and choir. With my George Formby friends I

Trade Fairs, Festivals and Street Entertaining

have played in café's, car parks and theatres in France, Belgium, Ireland and the Netherlands.

Language, Lavatories and Laundries

I often wonder how I came to spend much of my non music working life in the laundry industry. Having left college in the early 1970's and worked with my wife at TI, we both found ourselves casualties of the so called recession. We were due to marry, had bought our first house and life was full of future dreams.

In educational terms, I was a linguist, a "business studies" person and a marketeer. In employment terms I was an ex Commercial Apprentice, a technical translator and an office export sales clerk. In those days, the newspapers were full of jobs. The recession hadn't really bitten hard but as in my case it had begun to nibble away at hardcore British manufacturing. Looking back now, it can be seen that the 1970's was a decade of the death knoll for many UK manufacturers who, finding themselves in an inflationary economy, found their export trade hard pressed to compete. As an island, Britain had long survived from its healthy export business and UK manufactured product could be found all over the world. Exports were a major trade earner and the UK had been riding a high for many years.

Having bought our first home in Newport near Telford in Shropshire, relocation options were not attractive. We had been lucky to find a house we could afford. The 1970's had seen the creation of "gazumping" where would be house

Language, Lavatories and Laundries

buyers were outbid often at the last moment of the sale. Some even reached the solicitors office to exchange contracts only to be told that the buyer now wanted more money. We had been lucky. We had found a semi detached in Newport that was owned by a young family needing to move on for more space. The house had a happy feel and the sellers were genuine people who stuck to their word and their price.

It was therefore necessary to find a job withi striking distance of our soon to be home. Living in Newport offered new employment horizons, towns that were more easily accessible from Newport than Wolverhampton. By car, the Potteries and North Shropshire were easily reachable. Telford and Shrewsbury were on the doorstep. Wolverhampton and the Birmingham conurbation lay to the south.

The world of work was wide open to a young man with qualifications and a bit of experience. My only hindrance was perhaps how I looked. My hair was shoulder length and my beard full. I was not an unusual sight in my day but some employers were still very conservative. Jobs were in abundance and it was not long before I was offered a job in marketing at theWellcome Foundation in Crewe. The job was based at Crewe Hall, still owned by the Queen and leased out to my new employer. My long hair and "hippy" look ingratiated me to my new

Language, Lavatories and Laundries

employer who was looking for a young team with flair and imagination to help rebrand a subsidiary company. My bubble was slightly burst in that the subsidiary was named Calmic, soon to be rebranded Wellcome Industrial. Calmic was a service provider of kitchen and toilet cleaning and was known for the little chrome units that were plumbed into gents urinals and which gave a very necessary discharge of perfume in an environment known for less attractive odours.

I didn't know at the time but Calmic was to change my life in many ways. I was to meet there the best male friend I ever had in my life and I was also introduced to the service industry, not a big part of the economy then but of course to become huge, much bigger than manufacturing.

My new workmate and friend, Doug, was an industrial perfumier. He spent hours creating, testing and refining perfumes, in this case lavatorial perfumes. Later in life he became a very rich man but sadly died in his 50's of legionnaires disease contracted whilst on holiday in Greece. He was to out live his wife Helen who died of cancer. Helen was to become best friend to my wife Jill. We have never got over losing them. Their loss was a crisis in both our lives and our "grey" years have been much poorer without them.

Language, Lavatories and Laundries

My 18 months at Calmic therefore gave me my best friend and it gave me exposure to a very different world from my TI days. This was a fast moving non manufacturing environment and I was part of a small highy qualified and very young team. We rebranded , reliveried and relaunched to our hearts content. I was involved in product concept, design, test marketing, advertising, public relations. I wrote technical literature and I wrote advertising copy. Every aspect of my college learning was drawn upon.

Added to this was of course the fun of learning about the industry I was now in. I helped clean lavatories down a coal mine and kitchens in a London Hospital. I inched my way through overhead ventilation shafts (my potholing experience came in useful here as I did not suffer from claustrophobia) and chipped many a chunk of uric acid from a urinal ! I came home with dead rats solidified in solid blocks of kitchen grease and shovelled buckets of dead cockroaches that we killed with boiling water. My previouse experience as a labourer obviously did me proud here as I was able to work as hard as any of the regular team and I never remember any resentment arising from me being a visitor from HQ. I never found it difficult to win the respect of my colleagues and that was probably because nothing was ever too

Language, Lavatories and Laundries

unpleasant, too demanding or too menial. When you put your hand and arm into a toilet basin full of human excrement to clear a blockage, the people you work alongside , who have to do that same thing every day, watch your face and measure how you handle the experience. You become part of the team or you condemn yourself to being outside it. Thus the "rites of passage" in the toilet and kitchen cleaning industry were of "U" bend variety and second to none!

My toughest assignment was based in Scotland. I helped stage an exhibtion at Kelvin Hall in Glasgow where we launched a new contract concept to be test marketed in the Scottish region. After the exhibition, my job was to launch and monitor the product/service in a textbook test marketing situation.

The 1970's was a very different world to todays world. As I write it is almost 2008. The UK experience in the 1970's was very different. Fast food was still fish and chips. Convenience food was fish fingers. Pre 1974 McDonalds had still to open up in the UK. The concept of service was very subservient to manufacturing. Making things was still regarded as a "proper" job. Doing anything else was still considered from slightly unusual to unimportant. This was certainly the case in the Midlands and the North. The Black Country made iron & steel

Language, Lavatories and Laundries

and products made therefrom. The East Midlands made hosiery and lace. Merseyside, Tyneside and the Clyde were still manufacturing ships and serving the world with Britains manufactured goods. Most waterways in Britain were largely devoid of animal or fish life such was the level of industrial pollution. Britain was known as the workshop of the world. I was born into this workshop of the world but now worked for a company that cleaned toilets and kitchen! Unusual!!

Selling such a service was tough. Employers were too busy meeting swollen order books to worry about the state of the lavatory. Lavatories were almost expected to be foul smelling environments; that way workers did not dwell in them too long! Commercial kitchens were not subject to anything like the environmental health scrutiny that they receive today. A solidified dead rat could lie underneath a cooking range for weeks or months. Arguably it was not a health risk. It was embalmed in solid fat. Cockroaches could emerge from the drains at night and crawl all over the kitchen range for hours on end. The following morning everything was put right with pans of boiling water and a good scrub.

Years later I was to study and pass the Royal Institute of Public Health and Hygiene

Language, Lavatories and Laundries

Diploma. An environmental officer told my class how he would call in on food outlets and tell them he would be calling in to inspect later in the day. In his absence they would then clean like they had never cleaned before. Typically he would then inspect and record the presence of bacterial contamination as the basic principles of cleaning were not understood and cross contamination with cleaning cloths and rags was rife. Hence the reason why a dead rat may be argued not to be ahealth risk if fat embalmed. Difficult to understand but nonetheless true. A clean looking surface is not necessarilly a hygienic one!

The Calmic sales team in Scotland were selling a little wanted service and product range to a region not known for squandering money. My job was to retrain them. Their mode of selling would today almost amount to bullying. To get an order, they had to "tough" their way in, on an uninvited cold call, then bulldozer their way through the employers sentinels to put themselves in an arena where the buyer did not want to talk to them nor to buy what they had to offer. They then had to verbally ambush the buyer by a closed question approach to sign up. On top of that, the buyer had to agree to a years rental/ service charge in advance.

I quickly learned that without sales experience, I was not up to the job of retraining these people to sell a new service range. I took the bull by the horns and started selling, with them in tow rather than them selling with me in tow. Again, I was lucky to quickly earn their respect and the outcome was a successful test market.

Crewe Hall was an hour and a half each way from Newport. Though it was a great place to work it added three hours to my working day. The Queen's art collection which hung on the walls would be exchanged a couple of times a year and new paintings hung. The gardens were beautifully maintained and with my team of young friends it was fun place for a young man to be. Sadly, the team was headed by a manager who was less than competent. This has been a recurrent feature of my working life and now with hindsight I suspect much of it to be the arrogance of my own youth and later the arrogance of my own ambition rather than any shortcoming on their part.

It was to be the reason I left Crewe and also to become a salesman. I had concluded in Scotland that the experience of selling was to be an essential tool if I was to develop my marketing career. Somehow during this period my linguistic aspirations were seconded to the need to develop and prosper.

I was attracted by an advertisement in the Daily Telegraph for a salesman (age and experience

Language, Lavatories and Laundries

no barrier) for a service company operating in the hygiene market. With my background at Crewe where I had combined marketing and sales training with the launch of a lavatory cleaning service, I was surely to be successful!

In those days it wasn't difficult to be successful – jobs were a plenty. I was offered the job of a sales representative in the Midlands. It seems bizarre by todays standards but I was one of several and such was the level of industrial activity that a few Black Country towns more than kept me busy.

The firm I worked for was called Spring Grove Services (SGS) and in its day claimed to be the largest provider of rental polyester cotton workwear in Europe. Sadly, it exists no longer having being subsumed into the larger Sunlight Service Group. The SGS HQ was in Henley on Thames and I went on a one week training course. Although I didn't know it at the time SGS was the training ground for many people in the industry and for the rest of my working life I have encountered SGS people. The training was brilliant in as much as I never realised that I was now working for a laundry. SGS was second or third largest in the UK. It wasn't until I was back in Sparkbrook, Birmingham that the "laundry" penny dropped.

Language, Lavatories and Laundries

Being a salesman in the 1970's selling a workwear rental and cleaning service to a heavilly polulated heavy industrial area was not difficult. I found it great fun and was priveliged to experience many great British industries which sadly no longer exist. My patch was the true Black Country - Blackheath, Lye, Stourbridge, Dudley, Rowley Regis and Brierley Hill. In those days these areas were still employing thousands of people in traditional "metal bashing" industries. Sometimes I would walk along streets that literally shook with the cyclical pounding of drop hammers.

Part of my job involved measuring up wearers for thir new workwear. The Black Country dialect was still very strong but being a Bilston boy I had no problems. "'Ow B'ist", was a common greeting and it was my pleasure to reply (much to their surprise) "Bay too bad thanks". I delighted in the yows, goo's, cors, ay's and baints. The folk I was serving were proud Black Country "folk" and any attempt to link them to Brumijum (Birmingham) was met with contempt.

Language, Lavatories and Laundries

The Black Country was so named because of it's industrial past. It has nothing to do with ethnic immigration although today that might be hard to believe. Back in the 1960's and before, it was a heavy coal mining area and together with its heavy industry caused the whole environment to be blackened by its pollution. It is written in folk lore that Queen Victoria refused to look out of the window as her royal train passed through. The whole area was (and still is) cris-crossed with canals built to facilitate movement of heavy goods. Lye and Cradley were world famous chain making towns laying claim to orders such as the anchor and chains for the Titanic. This was the area referred to by Dickens as "obscured from light and foul of air". The Black Country was said to be black by day and red by night.

The laundry factory I worked from was based in Sparkbrook just outside the centre of Birmingham. I remember that there were a few workers from the Indian continent though this was well before the mass immigration of today. Birmingham today is a major centre of Indian and African communities but then it was still a largely English white city. Sparkbrook today is the centre of the UK famous "Balti Triangle" restaurant trade. Back in the 1970's I don't think the Punjabi Balti had been invented though there were a few ethnic restaurants.

Language, Lavatories and Laundries

I loved my job at SGS. I even had a new car, a metallic bronze Ford Escort Mk11, 1300cc saloon. This was terrific step up the financial ladder as I no longer had the cost of running my Triumph Spitfire (which I sold). The tax burden was minimal in those days and a company car was a real perk. Having said that, I remember carrying some "ContiPlas" (early plastic coated wood) on the roof. I had bought it between sales calls at the end of the day. I had to do an emergency stop and hadn't bargained for its slippiness. It came off the roof and thudded into the bonnet like a pack of cards, one after the other. The Escort Mk2 had a fluted bonnet which came to a point in the middle. Sadly mine no longer did and I was terrified that my employer would find out and sack me! No defences in those days , it would have been straight out the door. Except that is to say, that I had some how become salesman of the year so I had earned plenty of extra commission and was regarded with some admiration. Much of the commission went on repairing the car from my own pocket. The admiration I kept but it didn't pay any bills!

It was during this time that I was asked to survey the new town of Telford and produce a report on the opportunities that lay there for the services sold by the company I worked for. In doing this I came across an old traditional family laundry based in Shrewsbury. They were

Language, Lavatories and Laundries

still enjoying the cash legacy of serving the public with a van delivered laundry and dry cleaning service but expansion opportunities had gone as the domestic twin tub washing machine and retail based launderettes eroded market share. Many such small local laundries were forced to follow their bigger rivals such as SGS and explore the opportunities of rental textiles – workwear, mats and towels in industry and linen for hotels. This particular market had been pioneered by Initial Textiles who had set up an towel rental and laundry service. To identify the product to the user, thay had "initialled" the users name on the product. So was born an industry which by the 1970's had been the salvation for many struggling domestic laundries. Apart from Initial, there were a few large players with names such as Kex (industrial wipers), AIS (Allied Industrial Services, wipers and workwear), Sketchley, GIC (General Industrial Cleaners, workwear), Spring Grove Services, Advance Laundries (towel hire both in the UK and with overseas "franchises". Sunlight who now dominates the market was still a one or two plant business, yet to become the market leader.

In the Midlands were a number of small laundries all of whom sadly are now gone. Names I remember are Pelham Laundry (Wolverhampton), Wolverhampton Steam Laundry (employing up to 300 people in its heyday) , Repairwell Cleaners (Bilston), Lyndon Hire (Smethwick), Oldswinford Laundry (Stourbridge), Castle Towel Service (Birmingham), Cooperative Cleaners (Birmingham), Smethwick Laundry, NTS (towel hire, Dudley), Supreme Laundries (Wednesbury) and Lyndale Laundries (Birmingham).

South of Birmingham were Quality Cleaners of Worcester and St Georges Laundry also of Worcester.

Out in neighbouring Shropshire were Laundrycraft (Whitchurch, Market Drayton and Oswestry), Belle Vue Laundry (owning Lilywhites, Affords, Perfecta and the former Wellington Steam Laundry) and Salop Laundry. In earlier times there were laundries at Church Stretton, Much Wenlock and probably others too.

Beyond Shropshire and into Wales were Newtown Laundry (formerly part of the Lyndale Group), Laundrycraft (Llangollen), Afonwen Laundry (Phwhelli), Portmadoc Laundry and Eirwen Cleaners (Aberystwyth).

I remember these names because in some way they all related to the life I was leading or going to lead in the laundry & textile rental industry.

Language, Lavatories and Laundries

I left Spring Grove (eventually bought out by Sunlight) and went to work for Belle Vue Laundry as Sales Manager. In those days the whole linen hire market throughout Shropshire and the Midlands was dominated by Laundrycraft. Though based at Whitchurch, Laundrycraft were to become one of the national providers of linen hire with strategically placed laundries throughout the UK. Because of the dominance of Laundrycraft, Belle Vue Laundry, needing to expand had bought out a number of its local competitors but still facing a declining domestic market had elected to set up an industrial services company supplying and laundering workwear, mats and towels. This was to be my job. We named the company Shield Services though it eventually became Silver Shield Workwear Ltd. At first I sold our services into Shropshire but as we grew, the Midlands, Mid Wales, North Wales and the Potteries all came into our fold.

As much as I had enjoyed dealing with the Black Country folk at SGS, I now found great fun in winning business in the beautiful surroundings of Shropshire and Mid Wales. I never much took to the Potteries and to this day find it exceedingly difficult to navigate my way from A to B. There were some notable experiences as this is an industry which knows no bounds. Any place where people work is a potential customer. Obviously the dirtier or more unpleasant the job, the greater the need for protective clothing and a laundry service. Abatoirs, knackers yards, animal by products and hide producers were amongst the more "interesting" both in what they did and the affect on ones senses.

It was during my time at Belle Vue Laundry (it too eventually bought out by Sunlight), that Jill and I had our first child. I guess I was a workaholic and I was late to the hospital when our first born was delivered. Back in the 1970's, maternity services to Newport, where we lived, was served by RAF Cosford and so Simon our eldest son was born in a military hospital. To give myself some defence, It was not the practice of the day for a father to be at the birth and in a military hospital it would have been less possible. It was normal however for a father (to be), to be on hand, on the premises, to be there as mom is wheeled to the delivery room and to be there when she awakes from her ordeal. I was there for neither and have regretted it all my life. Somehow, I have always allowed work to interfere with family life. I have never been able to help how I am but I am sure the outside world find it difficult to comprehend.

Those times were very different to now. My wife had worked up until two weeks before giving birth (she too a workaholic). In doing so

Language, Lavatories and Laundries

she forfeited her right to maternity pay. I refer to us both as workaholics but that is perhaps being unfair. We had grown up in the austerity of post war years and knew that any achievements in life would be hard won. We both had a work ethic instilled into us by our parents. I remember Jill's dad accepting that to work on Christmas Day and Boxing Day was part of his job. I remember that my own mom and dad worked all their life. My dad was a roll turner in Tipton who eventaully became a roll designer. My mom always worked too. She cleaned and skivvied when we were young. Her employer was a headmistress who lived at Fightng Cocks. This was the treminus of the trolley bus from Bilston so easy to get to. As dad came home, she went to work at Wolverhampton Telephone Exchange. Later she worked in the Post Office and eventually they owned their own shop and Post Office, firstly in Lower Green, Tettenhall, latterly in Oaken, Codsall. My mother worked literally to the day she died. She had always expected to and thought nothing of it. The night she died she was in her late 60's. All her clothes were laid out for work the next day.

The 1970's was a time of home owning, carpets, portable radios, multi channel TV, man made fibres, sophisticated packaging, car ownership and added value sweets and savouries. We had grown up with lino, crystal sets, BBC, woollen underwear, greaseproof paper, tandems and sherbet fountains. Work was fundamental to life. We were probably the last generation where many folk lived to work rather than worked to live. Our life captured the period when the Forces Programme became the Light Programme; the Light Programme gave way to Pirate Radio; Pirate Radio gave way to Radio 1. As the economy of UK Ltd grew, so Brillaintine gave way to Brylcreem and mongrels gave way to pedigrees.

I was very successful at Belle Vue. Unfortunately, selling a rental product means that every sale involves spending a "balloon" investment to set up the customer with overalls towels etc. The consequence of this was that I was made redundant three times. Eventually, fuelled by my own self belief, I decided to have a go on my own. Thus, Wrekin Linen Services Ltd was born. Sad that as a marketing man I missed the obvious misinterpretaion of Wrekin and reeking. Initially we set the business up as an agent for Newtown Laundry in Newtown Montgomeryshire (now Powys). We recognised that living in Wellington (we had now moved from Newport to Admaston), we were well positioned to get non seasonal business in the Midlands and transport it to Newtown which was still a very seasonal Welsh town. At one time the laundry made greenhouses in the winter that were sold via advertisements in the

Language, Lavatories and Laundries

Daily Mirror. This was just to keep its workforce busy. It also took on distribution of office products throughout Mid Wales. At the same time both Portmadoc Laundry and Eirwen Cleaners closed. Whilst they released valuable business into the Welsh market, the economy of Wales was struggling. Newtown had one large employer, BRD an engineering company. Tourism was of a very limited order and holidays were still traditionally taken at the seaside (not inland). Newtown Laundry was owned by a chap called Roger Wood who by my experience, was a nice bloke. He had originally been a manager for the Lyndale Group and had had the opportunity to rent the laundry building and work for himself. The laundries full name at one time had been The Newtown Steam Laundry and Electricity Works Ltd. It still had a coal fired steam raising boiler (the only one I have ever seen) and at one time excess power was sent to the grid. It stood alongside the River Severn on Pool Road. The Welsh language drive had not yet begun and although it's Welsh name was Y Drenewydd, people still called it Newtown. The laundry operated at two levels. Water was drawn into the below ground wash house where incoming washing was sent by shute. My eldest son recalls sliding down that shute with the washing. The old black and orange vans could be seen all around the area often with their lights pointing upwards as the vans were so loaded with incoming laundry. Newtown Laundry picked up the contract with Aberystwyth University after Eirwen closed. Eventually they were to lose it to Belle Vue Laundry.

What Jill and I offered Roger was access to the Midlands and we were to secure social service and educational contracts in the Midlands. Constant throughout the year except when closed for summer holidays, the educational work fitted perfectly with Newtowns summer peak. Sadly, the loss of such work may have marked the beginning of the end for Wolverhampton Steam Laundry who having lost such contracts was eventually to close. The opportunity for Jill and I in Newtown was an eventual partnership. Sadly this never happenned and eventually Newtown Laundry was to close. This was very sad as it provided much needed jobs in the local economy.

We never shied from work. Jill would go out twice a week in a little Commer van with our son in a carrcyot on the front seat. She would call on every school in Wolverhampton collecting cooks kitchen laundry. Meanwhile, I would call on all the social service establishments in a much bigger six wheel van of the "Post Office" genre. We would meet on a car park in Wellington, unload her van into mine and together with our son, who's

Language, Lavatories and Laundries

pushchair was now tied in the back, head off for Newtown Laundry. I remember doing the journey once on my own, unknowingly having contracted mumps. I collapsed at the wheel and went through a hedge. We had to earn a living so somehow, we had to continue to make those deliveries. No time for sick and there was no sick pay for us to claim. Our first months income was £15 and our mortgage £65!

The absence of any partnership development was the final push that we needed to set up on our own. We rebranded our business Hiregiene Industrial Limited and set about growing a workwear rental business. We rented factory premises in Telford and together with a micro van and a couple of small washer extractors eventually built a business of some £400,000 turnover. We always struggled with cash as we always kept growing.

Along the way came our second son, Ben, and we built or rather doubled the size of a house near Newport in Shropshire. I took up karate and eventually became a black belt, joined a folk band and drove a couple of donkeys. Life "in the sticks", with animals, land and a young family was wonderful. All too soon it passes by and you wonder if you could have made more of it. Hindsight is a wonderful gift but at the time you do what you think is right and I guess only one's judgement can be criticised.

Language, Lavatories and Laundries

Eventually children grow up and go out in the world to forge their own path. Parents give what they can by way of upbringing and family skills. Hopefully we did ok. Certainly we did the best we could at the time.

We became as big player in the provision of service to the local food producing industry but times "they were a changing". Tighter legislation and EU rulings led us to believe that we would be unable to meet impending rules and regulations and we decided that the time was right to move on. We sold the business to Sunlight for whom I went to work. Part of what they bought they handed back and thus was born what was always intended to be a "job on the side" for Jill. We never knew it would eventually be another £1m business.

I started as General Manager and ended up as Marketing and Development Director for a division of Sunlight. I much enjoyed my time there but did not enjoy working away from home. I moved on to Brooks to run factories at Bradford and Batley. The temptation was that they had a closed factory in Stoke On Trent which they wished to reopen. The plan was that I would manage the growth of business in the North West down to the Potteries. Initially this would be processed at Bradford but then with Stoke reopened, a pool, of business could be transferred and used as a platform for growth in the Midlands. Brooks is now closed and even then, was struggling for cash. The Stoke plant did re open but long after I had gone.

During this time, my children did much of their growing up and I was a part time father. I regret that now but at the time it seemed proper to maximise my earnings and provide for the family. Ultimately it became too much and I left Brooks pretty much at the peak of my career. I expected to be able to pick my next job from a number of offers but I never allowed for the change in the economy. I was no longer an attractive proposition. I had earned too much and driven cars that were too expensive. They say that "the higher you go, the harder you fall". I fell and found myself out of work for some time. I kept myself busy but in many ways it was the period that spawned my mid life crisis. To grow up in a culture where work is king and then be without it is the most debillitating, depressing and self worth erasing experience I know. The wretchedness of not being able to pay a bill or provide for everyday family needs is exhausting.

Eventually, having done some capital equipment sales in the NHS, I was to secure a much lower paid position in the Civil Service (working in but not for the NHS). Based from home but travelling around and with a reporting base in the Liver Building in Liverpool, this proved to be amongst the happiest times of my life. I made good friends and was very competent at what I did. Sadly I was to be seconded into the private sector which I enjoyed less. I had one final move to a small privately owned laundry service provider to the National Health Service. Due to financial mishandling this company was to close and hey presto, out of work again.

I decided that enough was enough. I was in my late forties and becoming unemployable. I rejoined my wife in her fledgling business, took

Language, Lavatories and Laundries

up my music full time and to this day continue in this way.

Thankfully that period is behind me now and I am able to look back without too much pain. I have many regrets in life. I know I took many a wrong turning. I have lost friends through death and through simply being too busy. I have always valued work beyond most other things and I have learned that everything has a price. For every positive there is a negative.

My positives are two fine sons and a happy marriage.

My negatives are best left to my own private recollections.

Donkeys

What can you say about a donkey – well, it has big ears, four short legs and usually a bloated body shape due to it being an eating machine. Usually, a donkey has a visible cross on its back. Unknown to many is that the donkey has the best chin in the animal world – soft and relaxing. I'm no expert on donkeys but I am an expert on living with them as pets.

I always loved donkeys as a child, I guess most people do. Britain in the 1950's was a place where if you were lucky enough to have a holiday, it was probably taken at the seaside and that seaside would have donkey rides. Industrial towns "adopted" seaside escapes. West Midlanders headed for Mid Wales resorts such as Aberystwyth and Barmouth, East Midlanders headed for Skegness, folk from the Lancashire mills went to Blackpool, Yorkshire folk demanded of Scarborough and Bridlington whilst Londoners headed to Southend and Brighton.

If you went to a local carnival in town or a village fete, there would be donkeys. Riding a donkey at the seaside was the nearest that many town children ever got to livestock. Living in a Midlands town meant sharing ones life with

Donkeys

dogs (often whippets), cats and racing pigeons. Urban wildlife comprised frogs, newts, butterflies, birds, rats and mice. Smallholdings might have a pig or two or even a milking cow. Foxes were still a rural animal, rarely if ever seen in town, badgers were heading for apparent extinction (though they recovered) and any rabbit found near a town was likely to end up in a pot.

I guess that in many ways urban life during the 1950's begat a generation of children who did not immediately recognise lamb as a sheep, pork as a pig or beef as a cow. We didn't share our life with these creatures so we were naturally distanced from them. Unlike today, fast food did not exist and eating out was not something the working classes ever did. This was the generation of sandwiches being wrapped in an old bread outer (or greasproof paper) and a drink typically a third pint of milk with a silver cap, and orange juice with a gold cap or water out of the tap.

As a child a donkey was first known as an "Eeyore" . A typical donkey name might be "Dobbin" and I recall a pre school book about a creature so called. With the advent of BBC TV

Donkeys

came "Muffin The Mule" and as a child, I made no distinction between donkeys and mules. As the popularity of TV grew and filmakers began to capitalise on this new medium, films were produced about subjects that the mass population would enjoy. Typically these were romance, the war and cowboys and indians. In a cowboy film, donkeys were typically associated with Mexicans, used as pack animals or for riding side saddle, and mules were portrayed again as pack animals but also as stubborn "inferior" horses.

I never thought as a child that I would ever share my life with a donkey. That was to change in the 1980's after we bought a house near Newport in Shropshire. I was then in my mid 30's and life was good. The children were young, Ned (my alsation/whippet was still alive) and the house near Newport offered three bedroom living, one mile off road with an acre of land. The layout of land was such that just over half of it was a natural paddock, at that time with fruit trees (though not enough to be called an orchard). The house we had sold was a typical "estate" house and the first thing that was obvious to us was that I was going to need some bigger and more robust garden tools. No

Donkeys

way could I mow a garden of this size with a Flymo and extension lead. We intended to extend the house (which we did) but thought that the paddock area would lend itself to a horse or goats. None of us had any interest in goats and neither son wanted to ride.

> FOR SALE -"2 donkeys. Cleobury Mortomer. Must sell".

We made the telephone call and arranged to visit. When we arrived, the house was like a menagarie. The donkeys were owned by two eccentric spinsters who at that time had them grazing in the local church cemetery. They were there because they had simply run out of grazing space. We sat in their lounge awaiting the proprietary cup of tea or in our case coffee. A cockerel was sat on the settee back just behind our heads. Goats wandered in and out of the room and a lamb was asleep in a blanket on the open fire hearth. The two ladies had bought the house with a few acreas intending to be self sufficient. Unfortunately, they found themselves unable to send anything for slaughter so everything grew. The cockerill "trod" the chickens with a regualarity that had increased their numbers to excess, the sheep became, well

Donkeys

more sheep (there is no plural) and eventually they simply ran out of land. By this time they had become known locally as a last refuge for any unwanted creature and so the whole place was crammed with all sorts of livestock, in number far too many for Noah and his ark. By the time the donkeys came along the two ladies were renting additional acreage but never accounted for donkeys being eating machines. The donkeys soon deprived all other herbivores of food so something had to give. Fortunately, the local vicar stepped in, his ears having pricked to the term "eating machine". He promptly sacked his "garden maintenance" contractors who looked after the graveyard and offered a home to two homeless donkeys.

Sadly, he never accounted for a basic principle of life – what goes in must come out! Quickly the parishioners were complaining about piles of excrement on the graves of their loved ones and the disappearance of expensive flowers that were there "a minute ago". Some parishioners also felt somewhat intimidated by two feisty donkeys still in the growing years. An ultimatum resulted. Either the donkeys went of the bishop was informed. Clearly the donkeys had to go.

Donkeys

The two donkeys were a sight of beauty, both Jennies, both glorious grey with clear cross markings on their backs. We were informed that one was already sold to a gentleman from Ironbridge so we could only take the other. She was called Primrose and we quickly arranged to rehome her. She was delivered by horse truck to our home by which time we had secured the primeter fencing to prevent our new pet from escape. We took no account that this little donkey had just been seperated from its birth sister and she spent much time braying and generally trying to attract attention. The perimeter fence proved futile and she ended up in the kitchen. More importantly, she got stuck, twice. Unlike a cat who's whiskers determine safe passage of its body, a donkey is shaped very differently. It has spindly legs, quite a sharp equine head, big buttocks and a huge belly. Thus the front can gain entry but the middle gets stuck and the rear has no chance.

Trying to turn a donkey around in a domestic kitchen is no small feat. As yet we had not procured the necessary "donkey accessories" that proved necessary. We had no head collar, no lead in fact nothing at all. Using a tow rope from the car we did eventually extricate her

Donkeys

from the kitchen without any damage. Our fear was that she would kick out and damage the fridge or indeed break the kitchen units.

The house was situated in what was originally a sandstone quarry and was nestled just inside the rear cliff face which then swept around the house's side complete with an indentation which we called the cave. The next time Primrose escaped she came looking for us only to find the kitchen door shut. She trotted around the rear of the house only to get wedged between the cliff face and the house. Again it required much coaxing, forwards and backwards to prize her free.

Eventually, we concluded that her escapes were the result of loneliness. She had spent all of her life with her birth sister who sadly, we were to hear, had died having been in in collision with an out of control car in Ironbridge. We decided that we should look for a donkey friend to share her life in her new home. We decided against a jack donkey (male) to avert the possiblility of the inevitable foals which might be difficult to home. It is not an everyday occurrence to see donkeys for sale but we were lucky to find a "superfluous to requirements" animal in

Donkeys

Shrewsbury. She had outgrown the owners children who no longer interested her and Jill my wife, arranged a surprise "bought as seen" purchase for £45 which she was led to believe was the meat value (to the pet trade) for such an animal. I read quite recently that donkey meat is used in the production of salami in Europe and that UK animals can still be exported for this purpose.

Jemma, as we called her, was delivered one Saturday afternoon on the back of an open top "camping" trailer. She was as long and as wide as the trailer and was secured in place by ropes which remained taught as long as she remained standing. Her neck was roped to the trailer front and her hind quarters to its rear. Ropes passed around her frightened body and secured her at each side. How she had made it through a twenty mile journey is a miracle and we were horrified. Such a sight today would quite rightly result in immediate arrest and subsequent prosecution. I think the seller (a gamekeeper) realised our horror and as she was quickly released he was off.

Jemma quickly bonded with Primrose. Jemma was the elder by about two years or so we

Donkeys

guessed. Without knowing their birth dates it was impossible to know. Jemma was brown with a black cross. She was small, feminine and delicate with dainty hooves and a pretty face. Her only failure was in her coat. She had clearly been abused and as the seasons wore on we were saddened to see the many weals and scars on her small body. We always presumed such hard treatment had come from a man because throughout her life and to this day, she remained shy, even frightened of men. To gain physical contact it was always required to stand in their paddock and await the natural curiosity of the donkey to persuade her approach. Any attempt to approach her was met with an immediate retreat.

Primrose on the other hand was the opposite. She was a big donkey with tall grey ears, misshapen legs and big hooves. She was overtly nosy and would force her way into any situation with an obvious physical presence. I loved both donkeys dearly but Primrose carved a special place in my heart simply because of her friendliness. She spent her life at the paddock gate demanding company and would react to any human sound no matter how distant or quiet. Indeed each morning as Jill and I awoke

Donkeys

and whispered good morning to each other from within our snug bed in our brick house, out there in the paddock, Primrose would let out a loud bray. Her hearing was quite amazing.

She also proved a very capable mimic. The house was situated in the middle of a 2000 acre farm part of which was used for the breeding of pheasant. Pheasant were an everyday experience in our garden so much so, that we rarely commented on them. Primrose learned how to mimic them and very often we would be alerted to the "clicking" of a bird only to realise it was Primrose making the noise.

Primrose and Jemma lived with Holly (our Great Dane), Ginger (a tortoiseshell cat) and Champers (Ginger's tom cat son). Ned my alsation whippet died and for a short time we had two labradors, Sooty & Sweep. Sadly they kept clearing the farmers pheasant and eventually we had to find them a more "domestic" residence. Holly replaced two labradors. Too big and too lazy to jump any fences and much preferring the comforts of central heating to walks down a muddy lane, she was the perfect dog. She had a wonderful

Donkeys

life which apart from living with donkeys included snow skiing, windsurfing and water skiing. When we came back from any holiday or weekend away, the donkeys would always give us the cold shoulder and we had to win their affection. This was usually done with cream cakes and doughnuts from a bakery nearby our laundry factory.

I loved having donkeys but felt that they should have more exercise than a half acre field could offer. Also, being unshod, their hooves needed hard surface to wear them or face being trimmed by the farrier (something they never learned to enjoy). I began to take them walks on a head collar and lead, just like a dog. Donkeys of course are built to work and a one mile walk down the track did not dent their energy resources. Their incessant nosiness and "eating machine" biology meant that they would stop every yard or so to eat something or poke their nose into something. They especially liked brambles. They each had beautiful soft pink tongues yet they were able to strip a blackberry bush with ease. They would readily pull out yards of bramble from the thicket and chew it thorns and all. Young thistles and nettles were

Donkeys

also a delicacy though fully grown nettle was not to their choice.

I decided to drive them. In her former life, Jemma had been ridden by children and was at ease with a weight on her back. Primrose had arrived with us as an adolescent and had no experience of doing anything except eat. I decided that I would drive them. Newport had a local driving society albeit with an entire membership of horse drivers. One of these drivers was a local farmer and specialised in training horses to ride and drive. I approached him and asked if he would be prepared to train my donkeys. Not that I had considerd it, but he informed me that if he were to train them, he would need to train me too. I hadn't thought of that. In order to train them they would need to go "full board" to his farm for at least two weeks and I would need to visit after work to receive my training.

Having agreed to train them, it wasn't long before they were in his stables receiving their training. It was very funny to see them because of course stables have two half doors, set in height terms to suit a typical horse. The donkeys, being much smaller in height, were

Donkeys

unable to hang their head out and at best one might see two sets of nostrils pointing upwards from the door in the stable. Primrose was difficult to train. She was barely used to being taken a walk before she was on the end of a twenty foot lead being made to run around in circles. At first I regretted them going into training in the way one is upset when the children first go to school.

After being made to work "in a ring" she was introduced to "foreign" objects on her shoulders and her back so that she learned to be comfortable with restriction placed on her body. Her head collar was eventually replaced with a bridle and she then was accustomed to a harness around her stomach with two leather straps, one each side. Eventually, these would connect to a carriage but at this stage they simply dragged on the ground. The next stage was to attach the leather straps to a piece of wood which bounced along the field behind her. Finally she was connected to a carriage or buggy.

Up to this point she had been lead from the front ie she could see someone in front of her. She now had to learn to lead herself with command given from her rear, transmitted

Donkeys

through the reins and the bit. Initially one person would sit in the carriage and command her to walk on or trot on . Another, holding her bridle would teach her by rote what those instruction meant. So, at the command of "Walk on" she would be walked. At the command of "Trot on" she would be gently trotted at a faster speed. "Whoa" with a pull on the reins pressed the bit against the back of her mouth. This meant stop.

In a very short space of time she knew what to do. It remained then to teach her road sense. At all times it was imperative that she felt safe and secure. With her bridle on she could only see in front of her, the sides and rear being "blacked out" by blinkers. Her head was encased in straps. One went across her head, another across her nose and a third around her throat. Inside her mouth was the bit and beneath her bottom lip hung a curb chain. Her ears poked out of the head band from which ran up a central strap called a winkerstay.

Her frontal body was inside a breast collar which is what she pushed against. This was heald at the right height to her body by two adjustable neck straps. Attached to the sides of

Donkeys

the breast collar were the traces which hooked on to the cart or carriage. Each rein ran from the bridle through two large brass circles called terrets. These were attached to a pad that sat on her spine as a part of the collar arrangement. Underneath her belly was a wide inner through which the belly strap ran. This was called a girth.

Along the length of her spine ran a back strap which connected to a group of leathers called the breeches. Her tail hung through a rigid section called a crupper (cropper?). Various straps secured the breech to to the frontal leathers whereupon all that was left hanging were the two traces which of course attached to a cart, the shafts of which passed through adjustable loops on straps from the breast collar.

During training she had been introduced to the road. It was my job now to expand that knowledge and continue to build the trust that she had build up to date.

Donkeys

Jemma took to driving very easily. Having been ridden she was already used to carrying weight and to wearing that leather contraption so unfamiliar to Primrose. Whilst much smaller than Prirose and lacking her strength, she was calmer and used her resources more economically. Primrose always had a wild heart. Jemmas heart had been broken in a former life and simply resigned herself to whatever was to

befall her, good or bad. There were to be many happy hours

(With Simon and Primrose)

driving these two lovely creatures.

Firstly however, we had to get ourselves a cart. I spoke to a local fabricator and we designed a

Donkeys

two seater creation. It ran on moped bicycle wheels (which was fine until they punctured) and had no suspension. The seating arrangement was two plastic patio chairs with the legs cut off. It worked but was very heavy and had no give in its construction. It worked well enough to join the Boxing day parade of horse and carriages and being the only donkey created quite a stir, but then, donkeys always do.

The problem of course was that I could only drive one donkey at a time so I decided to try the two of them in tandem ie one in front of the other. This meant that whils the one at the rear was secure in its shatfts, the one leading had extra long reins and was only secured by leathers. As a driver I had two pairs of reins to command but that did not prove my undoing. My undoing was that they were used to living alongside each other in their paddock and the concept of one leading the other was strange.

As the calmer of the two, Jemma went in front and we headed off down the track. By the time we reached the road I was beginning to feel uneasy. There is a lot of strength in "Two Donkeypower". It wasn't long before we were

Donkeys

embedded into a wall, a mass of tangled leather with two donkeys scared and frightened. I decided that tandem driving was not for me and sought to buy another cart, one each. One came up via my friendly horse trainer and soon we were out with me driving Primrose and Simon my eldest son, driving Jemma.

Donkeys

Ben (my youngest son) with Jemma, Boxing Day 1991)

Donkeys

(With my elder brother Keith, Boxing Day 1988).

This cart had solid wheels (which would not puncture), well balanced shafts, a padded leatherette bench seat with backrest, a whip holder and a fine running board. Either donkey seemed to fit quite snugly into its design and it proved to give excellent and troublefree service.

Having donkeys meant that had to have somwhere to shelter. The natural shelter provided by the padock fruit trees was decimated as they ate their way through them. They especially liked the damsen trees. Damsen bark exudes a "treacly" sticky goo which they couldn't get enough of and sadly having eaten

Donkeys

the harvest of damsens, they failed to realise that if they ate the trees there would be no fruit in the future. We tried everything to save a few trees but to little avail as they pushed and ate their way through most things.

I decided to build them a shelter and in my ignornace thought that one made from wooden fencing panels with a currugated roof would suffice. They ate two of those!

The donkeys shared our life; a life of a young family with growing children. We had decided when buying the property that we wished to extend it. Extending doesn't really do justice as in fact we more than doubled the size of what we bought. Moreover, because we didn't want to increase our mortgage debt, we dicided to do it out of earned income and to do as much as possible ourselves. The result was a building project that took up ten years of our life. Building a house takes lots of skills and we mastered most of them. Early mistakes resulted in an overordering of materials and we decided with the excess to build a stable block for the donkeys.

Building it in their presence was the greatest challege. They stood in the footings, knee high

Donkeys

in concrete, knocked brickwork over, chewed wood. No matter how much we tried to distance them from the stable project, they somehow overcame our efforts. The most successful prevention was produced by our fabricator friends. They manufactered a portable interlocking steel rod fence where each section adjoined the other with a tubular connecting sleeve. Even so, by the time the stable was finished each and every section hand been pushed severely out of shape.

We wanted the stable to provide shelter on demand so our fabricator friends were required to construct double saloon style doors which could be pushed open but then self close behind. As such the donkeys could come and go as they pleased. The stable was split in two with a half height blockwork wall so that they could spend time together ot apart but always in each others company.

The stable shelter also provided a secure means of containing them when the farrier came. They hated him with a passion and in that they were the only donkeys he looked after, he was none too keen either. For some reason, Holly the dog loved the farrier visits. Normally a coward, she

Donkeys

would bravely enter the paddock and steal slivers of hoof which she would then knaw like a bone. They must have been a rich source of calcium or vitamin because they occupied her for hours (though the smell was awful).

Following the farriers visit, both donkeys would often race around the field on their new feet. Donkeys gallop in a very different way to a horse. Horses tend to look straight ahead or down. Donkeys do the opposite and gallop with their heads held high. Such antics make them look very silly and simply add to their appeal.

Driving the donkeys introduced many new experiences to their lives. They both lived in a grassy field in the middle of a farm in a hamlet of two houses nearby another hamlet of around five houses. All properties were accesssed via a private track and save for service vehicles such as rubbish collection, milkman and postman, they never saw traffic, litter, puddles, street furniture, bicycles, horses or even many people. They were once scared witless by the local hunt when their paddock was invaded by hounds and men in bright red jackets on huge triple size donkeys (horses).

Donkeys

Every time we went driving a new experience befell them. If I drove only one, they seemed to communicate on return telling each other what had gone on in the others absence. Driving Primrose one day along a country lane, a crisp packet was blown out of the hedge into her line of sight. She froze solid. One day she saw her first puddle. More importantly she saw herself for the first time (in its reflection) and clearly thought another donkey was underneath her. Once she heard another donkey bray in the far off distance and her ears pointed forward as we drove towards the noise.

Generally speaking, traffic did not bother either of them. We went up the High Street, along a dual carriageway, into car parks (even in a supermarket), through crowds of people, along empty lanes and through farmers fields. They experienced tractors, lorries, hot air balloons, horse riders and most other conceivable forms of traffic. The one thing they never got comfortable with were runners and cyclists (especially if they overtook us). Cyclists especially unnerved them,

Most people are fascinated with donkeys, be it for the religous angle or be it that they are

Donkeys

simply the most adorable creature. There are however limites to such feelings. Picking one's son up from school for example does not add much to his "street cred". For me, it was an opportunity to exercise one of the donkeys with a set destination in mind. The journey was about 3 or 4 miles but encompassed off road, on road, traffic, school "rush hour" pedestrians, litter, every type of road furniture etc etc. My son's friends thought it was great but he was not amused. The local vicar, was quite the opposite. I recall giving him a lift to church one day. I am sure he could have walked it quicker but he was very polite and I am certain the journey made it to his Sunday sermon.

My mother in law loved donkey drives. Anyone being invited onto a donkey cart is receiving a rare opportunity. To drive with a horse is unusual (unless you own one) but a donkey comes with that extra "je ne sais quoi"! She especially liked off roading, not in the way most people translate such words, but more a gentle journey through the immediate countryside, along tracks used only by occasional farm traffic and going nowhere in particular. One drive I remember went for a couple of miles along a single lane track and ended up at a hay barn

Donkeys

with nowhere else to go but turn around. Once we were out in the heat of the summers day, the adjacent fields parched and baked by the summer sun. Ahead of I saw a water cannon as used by the farmer to provide an artificial watering from the sky. It seemed harmless enough until suddenly and without warning it turned in our direction. Hundreds of gallons of water poured onto our heads. My mother in law was fit only for a wet clothes competition. Morevoer the power of the water was like being hit on the head with a constant sorm of large wet hailstones. Primrose loved it. She was hot too and the water was a welcome and unexpected treat. Soon, the single lane track we were on was like a stream and there was no choice but to sit it out. Eventually, the cannon turned again and we were spared further drenching. On this , Primrose set off again, a happy and refreshed donkey.

To conclude my thoughts on donkeys I would invite any reader to visit "The Donkey Sanctuary" at Sidmouth in Devon. Every visitor is welcome and it is an experience many people repeat time and time again. My own donkeys ended up in care at the Sanctuary. Eventually Primrose died. To use their terminology, she

Donkeys

"went down" and never got up again. Jemma, instead of being alone was already established within a larger group and survived the loss. As I write this, she lives on. She is heavily arthritic but receiving the best care possible. It was tough decision to put them both there and I wish had had not had to be so. It was however, the right decision, though the memory of their going still hurts.

One Man Banding Today

One Man Banding Today

"Sixty pounds", I don't believe it.

"Thank you very much" I thought. This was my fine for not paying a Congestion Charge as I entered Central London on February 13th, 2008. They even sent me a photograph of my number plate, as though I didn't not know it! Now the congestiuon charge may be understood to the inhabitants of London, but to me, well I took the Ken Dodd approach and assumed I was immune from the rules. In all honesty, though why I now wonder, I thought the charge only applied to inhabitants, people who used the inner city roads all the time. Anyway, I did't let it deflate my excitement over the month I had had.

February 2008 started with a corporate film in London. Called "Have Your Say", it was funded by the Central Office of Information to be used by the Electoral Commission to promote awareness of voting rights. I was booked via an agent called "Streetentertainers" and was required to be in London N1 at 8.30am on February 3rd. I had set off at 4.30am thinking I had plenty of time and had in fact hit London at 7.10am. Nonetheless, I was 5 minutes

One Man Banding Today

late arriving at the N1 Shopping Centre where the film was to be shot.

The camera crew arrived at about the same time as me and soon there were steaming coffees for all as we unloaded our various kits and began to set up for the film. It was bitterly cold and being at the open entrance to the centre we were in full exposure to the wind. Fortunately for us, it didn't rain otherwise it would have been quite miserable.

The storyline to the bit of the film we were shooting went something like :

" A busker, is setting up in the centre. He struggles to open a folding chair and is helped by a friendly passer by. He has an amplifier powered by a car battery and sets up his microphone to sing. He throws down his cap for donations and prepares to perform. Passers by notice he is almost ready and gather round to listen. Just then, another busker, a One Man Band, (me) comes along the street banging his drum, playing 12 string guitar and using various whistles, harmonica and other mouth instruments. The One Man Band is loud and interesting and soon woos the crowd away from the busker. He is very popular and on

One Man Banding Today

removing his top hat, soon fills it with donations. The busker shows his jealousy as the One Man Band wanders off, nodding in his direction as he does so".

We all had a quick rehearsal and the camera and sound checks were done. We ran through the "Call Sheet" to ensure we all knew what to do. Chalk markings were made on the pavement so each of us knew where to walk to and where to stand. The first attempt was frustrated as I recall by an alcoholic who wandered onto the "set" with his half bottle of whisky intent on being part of the action. The watching public loved it and many thought it was part of the show. Many gathered to listen to the busker (who was an actor with no ability to sing or play) or to listen to me, the One Man Band thinking that we were genuine buskers, which, though I am, apart from interlude moments, there was no opportunity to entertain.

The second attempt at filming encountered another oddball, this time a Preacher. He didn't seem to preach much but walked up and down with great enthusiasm. Eventually the film was shot just in time to avoid the police moving us

One Man Banding Today

on. Such events usually need a licence from the city council and it is important to stay within timescales otherwise another day has to be booked to finsh off.

The following week I was back in London to provide entertainment for Miss Stella McCartney (courtesy of First Choice Entertainments). She was attending her three "stores" within the Selfridge store in Oxford St, London. I was booked by Stella McCartney Ltd to "one man band" around the store in the vicinity of wherever she may be in order to divert some of the attention from her or simply to entertain awaiting crowds.

Her three stores were lingerie, cosmetics and clothing, all on differing floors. I was required to move between the three as required over a period of some 4 hours.

I used my SATNAV to get to the city centre store. It was not a good idea and seemed to get very confused. I attracted much attention in the bus lane and many swear words from the London taxi drivers. I could see where I needed to be but struggled to get there. Eventually I did arrive at the prescribed meeting point and was met by a charming and beautiful young lady

One Man Banding Today

who confirmed that I was indeed Woody's One Man Band. She directed me to the appropriate car park floor reserved for VIP's!! This was of course to provide easy entrance to the store. I was helped with all my kit and ushered through an anonymous looked "keypad" door into a VIP entrance area staffed with people preparing to greet and meet Miss McCartney. My car keys were taken off me so that the car could be moved as required. I was led into a VIP changing room and told to wait.

I used the time to tune up. I still had no idea exactly what they wanted me to do as the booking detail had been scant to say the least. I knew I was to wander around and entertain the crowds. I knew the crowds would include other VIP's, fans and lucky shoppers. I knew that they wanted me to personalise whatever I did by including Stella's name where possible into the lyrics of a song. I had some ideas about this. For example :

"Daisy, Daisy, give me your answer do, I'm half crazy all for the love of you" became :

"Stella, Stella, give me your answer do, my dilemma is being in love with you".

One Man Banding Today

"Won't you come home Bill Bailey" became "Won't you come home McCartney".

I had chosen not to sing any Beatles songs and as Sir Paul was in town divorcing Heather, thought it best to steer clear of Scottish songs in case the lady's name came up in horticultural reference!

My piece de resistance was a little ditty I had self penned which went as follows :

"Stella, Stella, let me be you fella, this is my dilemma, I'm in love with you.

Stella, Stella, you're my Cinderella, I'm no fortune teller, do you love me too".

It hardly ranks with Lennon/McCartney but it served me well.

Eventually my "dresser" arrived, the person who would decide which of the clothes I had brought should be worn. When working outdoors I always favour my top hat and tails and even though we were indoors, this was indeed the outfit chosen. I was asked to quickly dress so that I could be prepared for my "performance". Later they arrived with 170 "Stella" badges of the "I Love" and "We Love"

One Man Banding Today

variety. These were painstakingly pinned to my tailcoat.

The artistic director (I think he was called that), had a very precise view of how the badges should look and had them removed several times until he was quite sure they were correct. They looked no different to me but then I'm an entertainer not an artist. I bow to the skills and competences of everyone and as a person who's artistic efforts end at stick men, I make no claim on knowing what looks good and what doesn't. I have a very precise view oddly enough where my One Man Band is concerned. As an entertainer, I know what catches people's eye and I know what looks good. In the case of badges affixed to a coat, I give in gracefully.

The changing room was pretty much what you would expect I guess for a fashion event. There were large mirrors adorning the walls and a rail with various clothes on. I was alone in the room apart from the badging affair. Outside the changing room was the VIP reception area. Lots of people from Ms McCartney's team were there as well as key personnel from Selfridges. Everyone looked a million dollars and I felt very self conscious and extremely uncool.

One Man Banding Today

I know nothing about fashion. Part of what I sell as a Traditional One Man Band, is an image from a bygone era. I guess it really is from a range of era's. A top hat (with pheasant feather), tails, demin jeans and boots is an assemblage of odd items that somehow all fit together in the context of what I do. In this inner city world of haute couture, wealth and fame, I somehow felt rather dated and jaded. Nonetheless, that is what the McCartney team were buying. They wanted me to play the part of a street musician, an admirer of Ms McCartney; a person who followed her and admired her yet somehow was always under her radar. In changing the lyrics of songs, the audience were never quite sure whether I was a "stalker" or a hired hand. Even Security were perplexed and I was approached on several occasions and asked to leave the store. Fortunately, my "chaperones" were always on hand to rescue me and offer explanation. Of course, in that I had to cover three floors, it meant that "travelling time" was between McCartney stores and it was at those times that Security thought I had somehow wandered in off the street.

One Man Banding Today

On occasions, I even had my own Security. When Stella McCartney arrived at one of her locations, the area would be cordoned off, usually with me outside playing my unrequited lover role.

There were many young ladies around, everyone of them beautiful beyond description. I expected to see the skinny catwalk type but both the McCartney team and the Selfridges team were properly shaped and very pretty girls. Fashion seemed to me to be a young persons game and my advancing years made me feel very conspicous. The heady perfume smells were very pleasing and as I was mostly wringing wet with sweat, acted as a convenient cover for my natural body odours.

I was firstly escorted around the route and given my timings. They had to synchronise with those of my host to ensure that I was always in the right place at the right time. I had to arrive ahead of Stella at each location to ensure that I could sing my undying love ditties in advance of her presence.

Like most men, I have always felt a bit uncomfortable around women's knicker shops, (not that the Mc store should be called so). Most

One Man Banding Today

men, finding themselves in a sea of ladies underwear feel some discomfort. If you show too much interest you might be thought of as a cross dresser, worse still a pervert. If you're on your own, you are definately a pervert or shopping for the wife which seems to me to be two absolute extremes. I couldn't help but think of "Father Ted" from TV when several clergymen found themselves in the knicker area of a store not unlike Selfridges. They executed a military retreat from a very stressful experience.

Of course, like all knicker shops, this was called "lingerie" and I couldn't help but notice a vast array of brassieres, knickers and suspenders. The Mc store was on a floor of nothing but shop after shop of knickers (sorry lingerie). There weren't many men around and my presence, whilst amusing, was somehow at odds with this bastion of femininity. I did feel a bit like the proverbial "bull in a china shop" as I banged, whistled and strummed my way through this gossammer ocean of delicate fabrics and teasing designs of intimate ladies undergarments.

I tried not to think of Mrs Slocombe from the TV show "Grace Bros" as she would not have

One Man Banding Today

fitted in at all. This was an experience for the upwardly mobile. My life is Primark or at best M&S. This was Selfridges, London, second only to Harrod's in size.

A month later, I was sat in the coach station at Digbeth in Birmingham awaiting the first of three coaches to take me to Paris. The Selfridges gig had gone well and I had been rebooked to ply my one man band skills in the city centre store "Le Bon Marche", Rue de Babylon, Paris where Stella McCartney Ltd has lingerie and clothing stores.

I rarely travel alone by coach so a coach station was a new experience for me. My coaching excursions, though numerous, are of the group variety where one travels within the context of an organised holiday or with my George Formby friends on our annual outing somewhere in the UK or even Europe. I boarded at Wolverhampton and there met my first "jobsworth" :

"You'll have to leave that behind. Can't take that thing in the coach"

"That thing" of course was my One Man Band. Fortunately the coach driver was within earshot

One Man Banding Today

and said he would take it but that it was my responsibility and he couldn't guarantee that at London and onwards, future drivers would be so accomodating. As it happens, though none of the drivers that I met would ever be entered for a customer services award, no further comment was expressed as to my rig.

I travelled with National Express to London and then on to Paris with Eurolines. The first change was Digbeth in Birmingham. This was the new coach station and was only a few years old. I guess it was funded by the lavatory entrance fee which at 20p seemed extornionate for a pee! I can think of no other UK business today which thinks that part of their customer service provision involves charging a fee to use the lavatory. Having said that they were clean. They seemed the personal domain of a large African lady who patrolled them with a military purpose. Another passenger told me that this same lady had managed the lavatories for years. I admire that. Many might say that she had no ambition but I don't agree. I always remember working with a man who was Deputy Managing Director of a company. I once asked him if he looked forward to being MD. He replied that he never wanted to be MD

One Man Banding Today

but that he wanted to be the best Deputy that he could be. I guess the African lavatory lady was of similar mind. She enjoyed what she did, felt she made a difference and was so good at it that she was "above" the level of being told what to do. On reflection, if my 20p made this lady feel good about what she did, I don't mind. I guess however, that she earns national minimum wage and that National Express enjoy my 20p and those of everybody else.

It was at Digbeth that my One Man Band created my first travel conversation. It arouses peoples interest and natural curiosity. I was standing minding my own business when a Welsh lady told me she played the guitar. I wasn't quite sure how to reply and so just smiled courteously. She then introduced her friend and her husband as also coming from Wales. I told them that my daughter in law was Welsh and that she and my son lived in Wales and that was it , we were best friends, known each other for years just never met before!

Later, a young man joined me in the seated area and told me he could play a tambourine. Again curiosity took over and he grilled me on the intricacies of One Man Banding. I guessed by

One Man Banding Today

the paint on his trousers that he was a decorator. It seemed that he and his his dad were builders and decorators in Bulgaria and he too was waiting for a connection. I was due to arrive in Paris the very next day (Thursday). His journey was not to end until Saturday and then he was reliant on his parents collecting him from somewhere I can't pronounce.

I don't think you would travel on an aeroplane in trousers covered in paint and I feel this says a lot about coach travel. Everyone was going somewhere and many were going on holiday yet there was no sense of holidaymaking. There was nothing uplifting about the experience. Everyone seemed dressed for the long haul with little attention to fashion or design. This was utilitarian travel. Airports have shopping mals where you can buy almost everything. Ferries have duty free, bars, casinos and restaurants. Digbeth had a shop and a food retailer selling filled rolls. As I recall, on the outward journey, both were closed!

Having embarked on the journey from Digbeth, (Birmingham) to London, I was immediately hit by that scourge of modern life - the mobile phone. It seemed that everyone travelling felt

One Man Banding Today

the need to communicate with everyone they had ever known. The level of conversation was at times deafening. No sooner had one phone been answered than another one rang. It was 1645hrs when we left and shortly afterwards darkness began to descend. The mobile phone freaks then found new ways to use their toys. A couple of lads in front of me watched a film on their Apple phone whilst others used theirs to play music. I belong to that generation where a phone is for making and receiving calls (and only when you really need to tell or be told something). To these people, their phones were a hobby and the million things that a modern phone will do, they did. I am tempted to think "Get a life" but then I'm an old fogue I guess, a yesterday man.

I was asked by a young Asian man if he could sit by me on the coach. He was originally sat behind but could get no rest due to his co passenger's phone antics. When he sat down and closed his eyes I thought he was sleeping. Later in the journey he told me that he used coach travel to meditate and that involved constant repetition of 5 words. Each to their own of course but as a songwriter I would bore my audiences to death if that was the extent of

One Man Banding Today

my vocabulary. Then I know nothing about meditation. He was on a journey to London for a singles night of young Asian professionals. I found that rather refreshing after all the bad press I had read about arranged marriages and ladies having to wear (or choosing to wear) the burkha. I had even read about "burkha bandits" who used the outfit to conceal their identity in a life of crime. For £13 travel cost from Birmingham to London, this young man was spending an evening in the company of young professional Asian ladies and I guess was looking for romance. I hope he found it.

The change at Victoria Coach Station, London was efficient and on time and soon we were speeding through and out of south London and on our way to Dover and the Eurotunnel. Victoria was a depressing place. It was like a wind tunnel and offered few facilities. It wasn't especially clean but that said, it did everything it needed to, but no more.

When we arrived at Eurotunnel we had to wait for the next slot and were told we had 20 minutes to enjoy the facilities. These turned out to be one lavatory and four vending machines. I made use of each as did my fellow travellers. I

One Man Banding Today

noted that as per Wolverhampton, Digbeth and Victoria, other travellers were mostly ethnic. On my coach going out to Paris, there were only a handful of white people and some of those were foreign. It made me realise how the world has moved on. People clearly thought little of travelling two hours each way to London for night out! Many of my co travellers were African and had probably seen far more of the world than me. Some of them had no luggage apart from a mobile phone or a haversac.

The stop at Eurotunnel was the first chance for the smokers and when we all re boarded the coach, the stench of stale smoke was truly foul. The bloke behind me had a smokers cough and each time he hacked I was overpowered by his oral odours. Never the best experience for a singer; you have no idea what you will ingest (especiaslly when 40,000 of them are flying with each cough)!

I went to sleep on re boarding and awoke to find us flying through France. We had gained an hour passing through the time differential and in no time at all it was 6am and we were drawing into the Euroline Coach Station, Avenue du General de Gaulle, Bagnolet, Paris.

One Man Banding Today

We disembarked and in seconds everyone seemed to have melted into the dark Parisian morning save for two Chinese girls who were clearly as confused as me. At least their confusion was based on trying to read a metro map written in an alphabet that was alien to them. In my case, it was just lack of savvy, ignorance and the trepidation that has seemed to come with age.

Eventually, I worked out that I was next to a metro station called Gallieni. I had no sense of the compass but if I assumed the top of the map was north, then I was north west of the River Seine and was on the furthest westerly metro station of Line 3, the green line. I could see that if I travelled to Gare St-Lazare and then switched to Line 12 (which for some reason also looked green), I could then travel to Sevres Babylon from which the Rue de Babylon, my destination could be found.

My gig was at 6pm though I had been asked to arrive by 4pm for dressing. It was 6am and I had 10 hours to fill. I decided that if I got to the gig at Le Bon Marche (a department store), then I could drop off my guitar and One Man Band and perhaps make something of the day.

One Man Banding Today

My first experience of the Metro was very favourable. It was clean and clearly efficient. Trains seemed to run every minute or so and even to me it was not too difficult to work out.

The change at Gare St-Lazare was a bit of a hike with all my kit, but eventually I arrived from there to Sevres Babylon. I emerged up the steps into an early, awakening Paris. I worked out where I was and eventually found Rue de Babylon where I then found Le Bon Marche. It was now 0650am and I was dismayed to learn that the store did not open until 10am, another two hours. Every other day it was 9am but Thursdays was 10am. Just my luck! It was bitterly cold and nowhere was open. I decided to head back to the metro and escape the chilling wind but as I did so, the sun appeared and though cold, there were at least some shafts of warmth.

I had been there about 10 minutes when a van pulled up and a man asked me if I was going to play there. I replied "Non" in my best French. He then explained that he was a newspaper vender and I was stood on his pitch and he was licensed and it cost him money to be licensed – in other words "Shift".

One Man Banding Today

It was about this time that I saw my first tramp. He was ambling along with all his possessions in a collction of plastic bags. I was frozen to the core and guessed that if anyone knew a warm spot, a tramp would. I began to follow him (from a distance) and eventually he settled on a grating outide a shopfront. By this time Paris was awakening and folk were beginning to be seen on the streets. I joined him, at a distance, on the grating and found that it was an air conditioning outlet or something similar as warm air was drifting up from below. I was tempted to set my One Man Band up and start busking but was afraid of arrest and the subsequent failure to meet my contractual obligations. Instead, I just allowed the warm air to wash over me, especially my hands which were blue with cold. I realised just how desperate it must be to be homeless, to have nowhere warm to go, no basic amenities. As important must be the hopelessness and desolation that comes with no purpose to one's day other than to survive to the next.

When I was warm enough I thought I would check out the local "Repose" area that I had seen near Le Bon Marche and the Metro. These areas ar small grassed "mini parks" – a stretch

One Man Banding Today

of grass, perhaps a childrens play area, some well kept flower beds and lots of benches. Clearly they were intended for the local population plus shoppers and office workers. At least I could drop the OMB on a bench and give my back a rest. When I arrived I found that the city council did not unlock them until 8.30am and there was half an hour to go yet. I carried on wandering around aimlessly. The streets were awash with running water as council workers washed out the gutters and the pavements. The city certainly started the day in pristine condition.

I saw my first velocyclette shortly afterwards – those truly French battery assisted bycycles. I was later to see a whole row of them for hire :

I remember my first time in Paris back in the 1960's. There were bycyclettes everywhere. With the passage of time, like every city, the car has overpowered Paris and two wheeled traffic was now much less. Later I

One Man Banding Today

was to see my one and only bereted man, another statement of Frenchness. Paris was awakening. I passed a "Presse" shop. I guess the nearest we have to them in the UK is an Ironing Centre but usually, our shops have frontages piled with bags of washing. Here in Paris, the window was laid out with meticulous attention to detail. Little stacks of carefully presented personal items of pressed clothing with small price tickets attached. Much of Paris housing of course is appartments so it is likely that the demand for outsourced domestic washing and ironing is much greater than the UK where we are used to gardens and washing lines.

Eventually, it was around 9.30am and I thought that if Le Bon Marche opened at 10am then it was likely they would open a staff entrance at least 30 minutes before. Sure enough a security entrance was open and I piled through the door with all my kit to the dismay and concern of waiting staff. I introduced myself :

"Je suis ici avec Stella McCartney. Il faut que je laisse mes instrument ici jusqua quatre heures, cet apres midi".

It all sounded pretty good to me.

One Man Banding Today

"You are English" was the reply!

He checked his VIP list for the day. I wasn't on it of course but the event at Stella McCartney Ltd was so I was ushered to Miss McCartneys clothing area of Le Bon Marche and told to leave all my kit in a changing room there. I asked if it would be safe. For some reason, he replied in French :

"C'est Le Bon Marche" and clearly in his mind that said it all.

I had done a little research on Le Bon Marche. It was conceived by Gustave Eiffel, who designed the Eiffel Tower and it's ornate building, on the left bank, dates back to 1852. Some claim it to be the first department store in the world. It features constantly renewed fashion collections from over 40 top designers and had a new lingerie department (presumably incorporating a Stella Mc area). Like many department stores it boasts a large and prestigious beauty and cosmetics department as well as a renowned wedding boutique. Being French, it would of course have to have something to contribute to the French reputation for food and not surpisingly a gourmet food market, (*La Grande Epicerie*), stocks thousands of products from

One Man Banding Today

around the world. Its clientele was clearly VIP and as such it offers personal stylists and valet parking. It also contains a culture department hosting exhibits and a contemporary art collection.

I guess "C'est le Bon Marche" does say enough.

Having dropped my kit, I literally felt a huge weight taken off me. It was now around 10am and I had around 6 hours to kill. Without my wife, I was literally at a loss. She had been unable to join me due to workload committments at the laundry and so I was here on my own, feeling somewhat guilty to be in the most romantic city in the world whilst she was supervising the production of some 40000 sheets per hour through or laundry business.

I decided to walk the left bank and set off for Notre Dame. It took me a while to get there having only a Metro map for guidance. Situated on the Ile de la Cite, I was surprised when I arrived to find so many people already there. I

One Man Banding Today

could hear beautiful singing and decided to go in. A service was in progress and the lead chorister in an adult male choir had an alto voice very similar to Jimmie Somerville of Bronski Beat. The sound made my hairs stand up. I decided to light a candle for my mum. She was the least religious person I ever knew yet she always hedged her bets by lighting a candle at every opportunity. I paid my 2 euros and lit it in her memory. For some bizarre reason, I then photographed the candle as though to prove that I had lit it. I noticed a massive chandelier that had gently and professionally been lowered from the roof to enable refurbishment. I thought of "Only Fools and Horses" where Del Boy, Rodney and Grandad somehow managed to crash a similarly valuable item to the ground.

Out of Notre Dame I headed along the Seine past the Louvre (on the right bank) which must be one of the largest buildings in the world. Built in 1793, it houses the famous Mona Lisa. I should have

One Man Banding Today

taken the opportunity to go in as I was my own. My wife is not a lover of museums of or art galleries but somehow, on my own, I couldn't find the enthusiasm. I saw the Eiffel Tower in the distance. Finished in 1889 it inspired the UK's Blackpool Tower which was finished only four years later in 1894. I noticed that the Seine still has working boats, large barge style boats that carry sand and the like. Joan of Arc's (Jeanne d'Arc) ashes were thrown in the Seine. The "Maid of Orleans" was one of my childhood heroes along with Robin Hood and Jim Bowie. When she was burned at the stake she was reputedly only 19 years of age but in spite of that was an intellectual match for her persecutors who clearly feared her. Later her comdemnation was reversed and she was canonised to become Saint Joan.

I had lunch at Le Saint Germain on the Rue de Bac and later headed back for Le Bon Marche. I was directed to the event and reunited with my kit which not unsurprisingly was as I had left it. I met the team and my dressers began the long task of pinning over 170 "I Love" and "We Love" badges onto my tail coat. When ready, I was able to sneak a photograph is the dressing room.

One Man Banding Today

At six pm I made my entrance onto the floor of Le Bon Marche and then for the next three hours worked solidly between the Stella McCartney clothing and lingerie areas. Unlike Selfridges in London. There were only two locations here and they were both on the same floor.

I guess part of the reason I am booked is the quinticessential English look that I project. Not surprisingly therefore I am used to lots of photographing both on my own and pose shots with visitors. As well as myself, there was a close up magician working. He engaged small groups of people whilst I created a moving show advertising my employers name. At least three people sidled up to me and stole badges from my coat but I can never be sure as of course my mobility is restricted by my kit. As always, I broke a string quite early on. It seems the bain of a 12 stringer to quickly become an eleven stringer!

The Japanese love One Man Bands in fact they seem to love anything that is slightly off the wall. I had lots of photos with Japanese guests and one told me I was awesome and presented me with two plectrums.

One Man Banding Today

For some reason, one of my tambourines became dislodged from my right foot and I had to hang it from my left arm for three hours which was tiresome.

I think the French rather enjoyed the eccentric Englishness of it all and certainly my thump, thump caused many to dance and clap. I managed a couple of French ditties. One was my "Stella, Stella" song which had now become :

"Stella, Stella, me permet d'etre votre mec, c'est mon dilemme, je suis amoureux de vous.

Stella, Stella, vous etes mon Cendrillon, remarque ce vieux mec, je suis ici pour vous".

The other was a Raymond Froggat song called "Red Balloon" which is set in Paris and has a French verse which reads:

"Bonjour madame, bonjour monsieur, je vous voir dans le parc, mains et mans tous les jours,

Il fait bontemps aujourd'hui et les fleurs sont si belles,

J'espere qu'ill ne pleut pas et vous avez toujours l'amour".

One Man Banding Today

Both seemed to go down well!

One Man Banding Today

Eventually, the night drew to a close and I marched back into the changing area two pounds lighter. My badges were quickly removed and before long I was outside in the cold Parisian evening heading for the Metro. It was after 9pm and the bus back to the UK left at 11.30 from Eurolines at Gallieni. I found the Metro and bought my ticket. The Metro turnstiles have a waist height bar and a head height opening flap, both activated by one's

One Man Banding Today

ticket. In the morning, I had been able to use side doors, presumably for disabled and push chairs. For some reason these were now locked and I found that my OMB rig would not fit through. I got in quite a panic but eventually found out that if I went through bent from the waist so that my stomach and OMB rig were parallel to the ground, I could pass below the upper swing doors.

I arrived onto the station at Sevres Babylon just to see the train leaving. The next one was five minutes later. As usual, my OMB rig aroused much interest and with its flags of St George and the Union Jack probably gave my identity away. The train arrived and I alighted to be confronted by a busker singing a Willie Nelson song about a train called the New Orleans. All attention was immediately upon me and I was reminded of the film I had done in London the month before where my arrival stole the audience from a busker. Here in Paris, it happened just like the film as he just gave up when he saw all my kit and after a swift passing of the hat and bagging of the guitar was off at the next station at Rue de Bac.

One Man Banding Today

I changed at Gare St-Lazare and fortunately had no more turnstiles to negotiate. I was back at Gallieni in no time at all, well in time for the connection. I was desperately hungry. Although I could have eaten at the event, I always like to be seen to be working. As a hired hand , it is not my job to sip champagne and eat strawberries and canapes with the rest. They are always offered but my work ethic is such that I like to give my all in the hope that I will be seen as a "value for money" spend.

Again, with all my kit, it is not easy to negotiate cafes or shops so although there was a McDonald's nearby, I hung in and raided the vending machines. I was befriended by a Parisian Chinese lady who was clearly intimidated by the "hoodies" that were in the coach station. They weren't doing any harm but were dressed to intimidate and were generally quite tall. As with the outward journed most travellers were black or Asian and I ended up as one of only four white travellers. I was the token Englishman, there was my Chinese friend, a Japanese student and a Polish worker.

Soon we were speeding out of the Paris night and heading back for the Eurotunnel. I was

One Man Banding Today

somewhat surprised to wake up at Calais on the dockside waiting for a ferry. To be fair my ticket didn't state that either journey would be by tunnel and in that I have never agreed with the building of it anyway, I was quite happy to be returning by ferry. We were required to disembark the coach, collect our luggage and pass through customs. I was last, deliberately, because my OMB rig can be a health and saftey risk in a crowded situation as I cannot see what is going on behind me. I once tried fitting it with mirrors but they proved more obstructive. I have fitted it with a flashing light and a "Short Vehicle" sticker which does cause some amusement. The flashing light had caused much sniggering earlier in Paris as I used the Metro but it did at least inform people to beware.

The customs officers were fascinated and a cry of "Bombe?" filled the night air. I explained :

"Non, ce n'est pas un bombe".

Nonetheless, they examined it's every orifice with torch and some sort of detection wand. Was this my introduction to the world of "Sex, drugs and rock & roll" I thought?

One Man Banding Today

The ferry turned out to be full of students, mostly from Sheffield University. They seemed to have been on some sort of sports trip and were generally weary and quiet. Many of them sat watching childrens TV in the lounge.

It was good to have some English food. A bowl of Frosties and a slice of toast served me well. In deference to my visit to France, I also had a croissant and then headed for the "Duty Free" shop to buy some perfume for my wife.

We entered Dover with the rising of the sun. It was a stunning morning and the white cliffs were resplendent in their cloak of early morning sunshine. There were no bluebirds but then there never were. Bluebirds are symbols of cheeriness, happiness, health and prosperity. The cliffs must have been a wonderful sight to those lucky few who returned from aerial skirmishes with the Luftwaffe back in the 1940's. They were a wonderful sight for me and I had only been away two days and my only enemy had been the cold and the Metro gates.

When I arrived back in Wolverhampton Coach Station, it was uplifting to see my wife waiting in the car. Going away is full of expectation but returning is awash with the comfortability of

One Man Banding Today

the known. Travelling on one's own is a lonely experience and I admire those that find a purpose in it.

My One Man Band had survived another endurance test – coach luggage lockers, Metro gates and a three day trip. Nothing was broken, everything intact.

I have no idea where my One Man Band will take me in the future. At the time of writing I have 40 plus gigs booked for the rest of the year including festivals, fairs, carnivals, a wedding and of course my old folks and retirement schemes. My next gig is with the Salvation Army. I have no way of knowing if Stella McCartney Ltd will need my services again or when I will next play abroad.

With my One Man Band and with my George Formby Society ukulele friends I have been lucky enough to play in Tenerife, France, Belgium, Holland, Isle Of Man and Ireland as well as all over the UK. I have played for holiday companies, religious groups, the British Legion (in France) and have appeared on stage, in film, in store and on the street! I'm not famous but I have had some fun.

One Man Banding Today

The future will reveal itself in its own good time.

The bluebirds are in sight!

Thanks for reading.